AN INTRODUCTION TO GROUP WORK SKILL

Fred Milson
Head of Community and Youth Service Section
Westhill College of Education, Birmingham

Routledge & Kegan Paul
London and Boston

First published in 1973
by Routledge & Kegan Paul Ltd
Broadway House, 68–74 Carter Lane,
London EC4V 5EL and
9 Park Street,
Boston, Mass. 02108, U.S.A.
Printed in Great Britain by
Ebenezer Baylis and Son Ltd
The Trinity Press, Worcester, and London

ISBN 0 7100 7645 2 (C)
ISBN 0 7100 7646 0 (P)

Library of Congress Catalog Card No. 73–80375

To Andrew
in pride and joy

Contents

1 Group work for everybody

What is a group?

In the broadest possible sense, a human group is a number of people who have something in common. So all those people in Britain whose annual income is over £25,000 form a group, as do the men and women on the earth who have passed their hundredth birthday, or all the red-headed people in Yorkshire. But clearly these people do not constitute a group in the sense that the members of a darts' team in a local pub are a group. So our definition already proves too broad; it is a blunt tool and not adequate for the group worker.

Different kinds of groups

The main differences between, say, the group of red-headed people in Yorkshire and the local darts' team are immediately obvious:
(a) The darts' team is small.
(b) They are constantly meeting and they have an opportunity of developing personal relationships with each other. C. H. Cooley coined the term 'primary group' for that human association where relationships are based on interaction. 'The red-headed people of Yorkshire' never meet together; they have no opportunity of making friends with one another; they are too large anyway to form a comprehensive network of relationships; they represent only a statistical reality.
(c) The darts' team have a goal—to win matches—which requires a contribution from each individual member.[1] If Joe is 'off-form', the match may be lost and his status and popularity with the rest can suffer loss. Not all small groups share a common goal which calls for an individual contribution from each member; they may be a small group, present together and having in common the same purpose for themselves, but not needing each other—and in this case there will be less interaction between the members and less group feeling. If six people are travelling upwards in a hotel lift, though they are thrown together and all intent on the same purpose, they do not need each other and hence they may not speak to each other. But if the lift is jammed between floors, they

may form a working party to extricate themselves from the predicament. Then they become a group in a different sense; there is co-operative effort on behalf of all; leaders will emerge; they will talk more to each other; they will feel they 'belong' to each other and the group will have an 'identity'.

It is easy to imagine comparable situations where a similar change takes place: eight people are travelling together in a railway compartment. They have much in common; for example, they are all travelling at the same time to the same destination. But for this purpose, they do not need each other and hence they remain strangers, not talking to each other, hiding behind their newspapers, concentrating on their books, dozing or staring idly through the window. A sudden collision on the line changes the character of the group. One of their number is buried in the debris and the rest organize themselves into a rescue party, with roles assigned to each in a joint effort and with much talking between them. Likewise, a group of spectators at the zoo watching the tiger in a cage have much in common. They are in the same place, doing the same thing; they may even share their delight, strangers though they be; but they do not need each other for their purposes. If a family leaves the group to watch the monkeys, the rest can contrive to admire the tiger. But again, let us imagine a crisis situation. The tiger escapes from the cage and the knot of spectators run to a nearby refreshment hut. Barriers have to be erected hastily; children to be helped and protected; now there is work to be done by each on behalf of all.[2]

This lengthy and imaginative excursion has been thought necessary so that the reader can be quite clear at the beginning what this book is about. We are here concerned with the behaviour of people in groups which meet fairly regularly, which are small enough to provide opportunities for every member to know every other member as a person, and where there is a goal to be achieved which calls for a contribution from each. (It is common practice among sociologists to call 'a social group' those human associations which satisfy the first two criteria whilst keeping 'group' for those human affiliations which may be vast organizational structures or merely statistical aggregates. Some writers require the third condition—a shared goal which demands individual effort in co-operative endeavour—to merit the title 'social group' or to be the subject of the enquiry known as 'group dynamics'. It is in this latter sense that the term 'social group' is most frequently used throughout the present work.)

Reasons for the current interest in group work

Although we may not have the remotest professional connection with group work, most of us are aware, even if vaguely, that 'group' (and its derivatives) has become very much an 'in-word' in this century and particularly since 1939. Perhaps we realize also that vast sums of money have been provided, particularly in the USA, for research into group behaviour.

A further enquiry into 'what we know already' will reveal to us that these researches were motivated by the desire to understand the psychological conditions into which service personnel were thrown; to improve selling techniques; and to comprehend work situations and hence, to increase productivity. But these may be said to be the catalysts, the immediate motivations for interest in group dynamics; behind them lie issues of long standing which in modern, developed sophisticated countries like Britain, West Germany and the USA, predictably focused attention on group behaviour.

First, there was an emphasis in psychology on the social aspects of the growth and development of personality. This is a long story which need not be told here in full. It is sufficient to say that in this century, powerful and persuasive voices have been saying that a human personality is very much a product of interaction with social environment. Of course, 'social' psychology is not new; perhaps it was from the beginning inherent in this intellectual discipline, but the fact remains that many of the early experiments treated the individual as an isolated unit, ignoring his social setting. In our period much has been said to redress the balance through the writings, say, of Lewin, Mead and Cooley.

Second, there was the realization that modern conditions often break up the old forms of human association and make it necessary to create new groups for people to belong to and this demands knowledge of how groups work. Again, we are telescoping a long argument here; we cannot justify it except by references for further reading. But in briefest form the case runs as follows.

Until recently, most people living in these islands belonged to relatively small, close-knit communities; they worked in small units; they did not move far away from where they were born; they did not usually rise above the social class in which they were born. Their lives may have been restricted and prescribed, but they knew where they were, had a sense of belonging and a recognized place in a community. By contrast, in a modern, urbanized, overpopulated, industrialized, mobile (both geographically and socially) and rapidly changing country like Britain in the 1970s, the individual may have more freedom and opportunities for self-advancement, but he has less sense of belonging; he is more isolated from his fellows. We are often told that in many parts of the country, the old community feeling has gone.

The logic of this state, accepted by group-minded social philosophers, is that, since even in modern conditions we still need each other ('Normal people grow in the soil of group life, deriving from it the mental and spiritual chemicals of growth'),[3] and since in a rapidly changing society groups do not always easily grow, we have often today to create artificially, that is by social engineering, the groups which before usually developed spontaneously; since groups for the vast majority are still necessary for happiness, fulfilment, security and welfare.

Third, there was the realization that many tasks, important to us, are better achieved by group effort than by individuals working on their own. Two things should be noted here: first, that this is not a new truth which had to wait until the twentieth century to be discovered. Men have long appreciated the value of team effort in, say, sport—and that is to mention only one realm where hundreds of examples could be quoted. What was new—as we shall see—was the recognition of the efficiency of group affiliation in previously unrealized and unsuspected areas. The second point is that 'group methods' may be efficient for 'bad' purposes as well as 'good'. To a degree, they can be used by the 'indoctrinator' as well as the 'educator'. (And they are often used by the 'indoctrinator' who thinks he is an 'educator'.) But the following illustrations of the practical use of group methods are confined to what most people would regard as 'good purposes':

(a) *Group psychotherapy*[4]   In a mental hospital where there was a shortage of analysts, it was discovered that patients could be encouraged to talk through their problems in group situations. Under skilled leadership, they were encouraged to bring their repressions into the open, only to find that they were still accepted by the group. Attempts have been made to extend the use of this method for disturbed and delinquent youngsters and also in the rehabilitation of prisoners.

(b) *Group work in social work*[5]   To put a large matter briefly—
the old image of the social worker as being involved with one client
in an interview has been modified by the recognition that the
client can only be understood as belonging to a number of small
groups, like the family. The social worker must be aware of these
pressures and opportunities in order to help the client to help
himself and come to terms with his own problem. Hence more and
more courses of training for social workers include group work
skill.

(c) *Groups for learning*   It has been realized that many subjects
can be studied better by the involvement of a whole group of
people rather than by relying upon one teacher or lecturer for all
the information. A good example of this method has been recorded
by A. K. C. Ottaway.[6] Students were recruited in the extra-mural
department of Leeds University for a course in the study of human
behaviour. Despite a careful wording in the prospectus of the
course, they came expecting to have a course of lectures in psychology; instead they found they were expected to use their own life
experiences to help one another to understand the springs of
human action. And despite early reluctance, and continuing
resentment, this method proved to be more successful. It could be
said, of course, that the subject of psychology is peculiarly fitted
to this kind of treatment; and it is true that there are other subjects
where a more decisive part can be played by the teacher who is an
information-giver since he has devoted himself to this subject.
But the fact is that more and more people have come to feel that
group methods are relevant to the school classroom situation, and
not only in the primary school—where social education is paramount—but in the secondary school too where the 'subject'
becomes more important. A teacher is often throwing away a
major part of his assets if he does not use the resources of the
group for the education of each member of the group.

(d) *Groups for training*[7]   The argument for mobilizing the resources of all in the interests of each is stronger still when the
purpose is not 'to educate' but to train in a skill which involves
working with other people, as in the case of social workers of all
varieties, teachers and industrial personnel officers. For there is
again the same factor that one then has a broader base for the
training of each, more experiences to draw upon, the insight into a

problem of more than one person. In any instance of understanding a human situation, it is overwhelmingly likely that fifteen people together will have more insight than any one on his own, however experienced and expert that one may be. But there is an even more important consideration where the subject of the exercise is the training in the skill of human relationships. Such students are not merely learning techniques; they are passing through a process of personal development where it is necessary for them to come to terms with themselves, their anxieties, weaknesses, insecurities and motivations. And these things are best learned in a group where the members can be more and more open with one another, as they learn to trust the group. Perhaps this personal development can only be achieved in such a group.

Many kinds of group workers

We have looked at some of the reasons for the present-day interest in groups and indicated one or two areas where this interest is worked out in practical terms. But in order to make the point, we have in fact concentrated on those people for whom group work is almost entirely the whole of their professional role—like the group-psychotherapist—or those for whom group work forms a big part of their professional role—like social workers (unless they are group specialists). This leaves out two important people and as this book is mainly directed to them, we ought to say at once who they are.

First, there is the man in the professional role where group work is a minor part of his method. Indeed, it may not have occurred to him that he is a group worker. Clergymen, managing-directors and headmasters come into this category. It is still common to think of leadership as being the personal influence which one man brings to bear on another; but in fact there are very few leaders who are not group workers, relying on more than their personal relationship with each follower and challenged to mobilize the resources of the group. In my observations, the failure of leaders to be good team workers is one of the major reasons for the ineffectual working of democracy. They often insist on giving individual performances; they see themselves as soloists, not members of a choir. But we can be more specific than broadly saying that many leaders suffer from a faulty definition of their role. They work with a one-way system of communication.

They do not listen to their colleagues; they fail to share information and goals with others; they hesitate to designate real authority and thus allow a large part of the 'plant' to be unproductive since they do not use all their resources; they have an undue reliance upon the prestige of their office. We repeat that practically every leader in the land is or is required to be a team worker in at least a part of his job and therefore we claim that the study of groups and the training in social group skill has a wide application.

But we are no less concerned with the exercise of group skill in non-professional roles, that is, roles that have nothing to do with the job for which we are paid. Most of us spend a large part of our lives in this way, as a member of a family, as one of a group of friends, playing regularly for a football team or attending committees.

It can be happily conceded that in all these and in comparable situations, some people display a high degree of intuitive skill. Many a mother, who has never heard the phrase 'group dynamics', still manages to be a successful group worker. Nevertheless, it is often the case, that in this as in other matters, what we do naturally on the basis of temperament and experience, we may do much better, by giving thought to what is involved and undergoing a little training. A young cricketer displaying natural talent on the village green may be taken to the county headquarters and taught the correct techniques. This may even for a time 'ruin his game', but in the end he will integrate inborn gift, experience and correct technique into a natural rhythm of effective stroke play. In like manner, the first impact of a study of groups can be to increase self-consciousness. But in the end one becomes usefully aware of the total situation and spontaneity returns but with added understanding and skill.

This is, then, definitely a book for the non-specialist—for mothers and fathers, and foremen and committee members, among others. That is why throughout it avoids the use of technical terms where more familiar words are adequate to convey the correct meaning.

Group work and democracy

Group understanding and skill are far too important to be left to the specialists. We need a diffusion of this insight and ability rather than its concentration among fewer and more efficient experts. Without being too sanguine, we could see a wide distribution paying rich dividends for our personal and community life. There would be less bullying; sensitivity would grow; fulfilment would often replace frustration; democracy, becoming more efficient, might become viable.

2 What is happening in groups?

You are here

There are cities in the British Isles which provide a useful service for the stranger, and also for the local inhabitant who is not too familiar with the locations of streets and buildings. Large street maps are attached to lamp standards; moreover, a prominent arrow bearing the inscription 'You are here' indicates the precise location of the lamp standard. All of which is very thoughtful, since the first requisite for any journey is to identify the point from which you start.

As we begin our journey to the understanding of group work, perhaps there is profit in a brief use of the same procedure. There are three parts to the reality which could be called 'civilization' or 'the human story', or 'the culture which distinguishes man from the rest of the animals'. These are:

(a) *Man's response to beauty* Here lie all the arts, the poetry that has been written, the music that has been composed, the buildings that have been erected and the pictures that have been painted.

(b) *Man's growing knowledge of the forces of the physical universe which is his home* The first hunter to turn farmer is in this tradition as are the inventors responsible for colour television. In this area lies the growing scientific knowledge and the uses to which it is put, which today we call technology.

(c) *Man's understanding of himself* It is the third strand which we have in mind when we talk about 'the social sciences'. Psychology, history, sociology, anthropology, economics and politics are examples. And as in the two earlier examples, we are concerned with knowledge and activity; theory and practice. In the social sciences there are academics whose primary function is to add to our total knowledge. Their role is to be social thinkers rather than social reformers or social workers. They may even have to resist the temptation sometimes to become too involved with the day-to-day affairs of man, since their purpose and justification is to see what is rather than to say what ought to be. By contrast, there are those who work with people who, presumably, guide their actions by the established findings of the social scientists. A generic title which has been given to all those who are occupied in this way is 'community worker'. It is deliberately broad. The intention is to describe those roles in a society where the main 'raw material' is human; where the person described is working primarily with people, and not primarily with ideas or non-human realities like machinery or animals. And almost always, the term refers to a worker who is working, it is believed, for the betterment, in some way, of the human beings with whom he comes into contact; or, to put the matter another way, he seeks to influence their behaviour beneficially. It is clear that under this 'umbrella definition' many occupations gather, including teacher, social worker, tutor and mother.

And now at last we can attach our 'You are here' arrow. Group work, of course, belongs to the third category. Its knowledge is rooted in the social sciences; it is supported by the findings of careful researchers who have studied group behaviour. On the practical side, it refers to the skill which may be acquired by those who want to influence the behaviour—presumably for their betterment—not of single individuals or of whole communities, but of small groups of people who meet together for a purpose.

Opening our eyes

It may seem trite to remark that seeing and hearing are selective acts; that in fact, to a marked degree we see and hear what we want to see and hear. This reality can be observed every day of the week. Yet training in group understanding and group skill begins by giving full recognition to this obvious fact.

Perhaps it is worthwhile asking why any one of us sees and hears some things, and not others, though what passes unnoticed may be glaring and loud. Sometimes it is an aspect of a personal relationship. In a buzz of conversation in a living room during the evening, a mother will hear her baby cry or even stir in his sleep when the others hear nothing. A man will recognize a close friend at a great distance but have trouble identifying an acquaintance at a shorter distance.[1] What we see and hear may reveal our own value-system, telling others what is most important to us among all the goods and services we may choose. There is the highly moral tale, often told, of two men passing some shrubs in the broad flower-bed of a city hotel. One heard the chirp of a cricket; the other did not hear it, neither apparently did any of the other passers-by. 'That', said the one who heard, 'is because you are not tuned-in to the chirp of crickets; but you are tuned-in to other sounds.' At this, he bounced a coin on the pavement, and with the metallic ring, half-a-dozen pedestrians halted in their tracks! Similarly, if four men undertake a long car journey through the English countryside, and afterwards give their own account of the journey, one may comment on the performance of the engine, another may have noticed the possibilities of landscape-gardening, a third has had an eye for ancient buildings, whilst the last man looked for the public houses. Clearly perception relates to interest.

Group skill begins by fostering our interest in group behaviour, in ways that will presently be suggested. This interest then passes by trained observation, and reflection and practice of the skill into a sharpened perception and a heightened awareness of people's behaviour in small groups. Colloquially expressed it is having a 'nose' for or a 'feel' for group behaviour. Insight is more important here than knowledge. Occasionally, on a full-time course of training in group work, one encounters the student who reads many books on the subject, and acquires a new vocabulary of exotic terms. He can verbalize beautifully about group dynamics; give lectures at the drop of a hat on the prominent theories; but he cannot tell you what is happening in a particular group to which he belongs. He represents a notorious failure both for himself and his tutor.

In encouraging interest in group behaviour, we are only asking people to look at life, to see what is there in fact, though often lying below the surface of popular observation. Of two men who have enjoyed a party, one remarks on the quality of the food and drink; the other may have been struck by the skill of the hostess, not only in helping to make everybody feel welcome, but in involving a lot of her guests in contributing to the general enjoyment; the successful hostess in fact has group skill as part of her accomplishments. Like many others—including, as we have suggested in chapter 1, parents, foremen and teachers—the hostess is a group worker though she, like many more, may not recognize herself under that title.

The fact is that most of us spend much of our time in groups; most of us begin life in one; most of us also during our adulthood frequently do our work in groups. In pleading for a heightened awareness of and deeper sensitivity to group behaviour we are simply asking that people should be more aware of the total human situation and at greater depth.

The following example, provided by Joan Matthews,[2] is a good illustration of perception and awareness based on interest, of group behaviour. It is taken from an incident in a youth club. There are two accounts of the same events. But the first is a flat, one-dimensional narrative; it is factual and accurate, but it never penetrates below the surface. In the second rendering, we find the observer aware of more of what is happening between the actors in this little drama.

> (a) Jim and Mike and three others spent three-quarters of an hour at table tennis. Jim and Mike are good players, and Jim wants to arrange a tournament. Bill was with this group. He is a poor player and was a nuisance most of the time, running off with the ball, etc. Jim became angry with him and threatened to box his ears. When the others had left the table Mike took Bill back and tried to teach him some good shots.

> (b) Jim, Mike, A, B and C, get a lot of satisfaction and enjoyment from table tennis, and like to play seriously. Jim is very anxious to establish his superiority in the game. He wants to be appreciated by others, but does not shine in the club as a whole as he is usually too self-conscious to participate fully except when he knows he can excel. Mike is more mature, and much more secure. He can tolerate competition and even distraction. Bill is socially backward compared with the other members, and seems to have no close friends. He very much needs to be accepted by some of the others, but expects rejection all the time, because he has no accomplishments. He tries to avoid this rejection by playing the clown every time serious participation is called for. His reaction to Mike's gesture of acceptance and help was well marked. While Mike was giving him his whole attention, and for a while afterwards, Bill was attentive, co-operative and much quieter than usual.

When those two accounts of the same episode are compared, we can observe that the second shows, at several levels, a greater awareness of what is happening to those people. First, the 'three others' of account (a) become 'A, B and C', the letters presumably standing for their names. They are then, in this account, not indistinguishable members of the club, but individuals different from all others, an acknowledgment which is symbolized by the use of their names. Second, account (b) penetrates below the surface of what those people do; it is not like the first account, merely one-dimensional; it tries to see why people are behaving in this way in the presence of others; what emotional needs, say for acceptance, security, status, self-confidence, are they seeking to satisfy in the group? And we notice that some are more dependent upon the group for emotional satisfaction than others. So Mike is cast for the role of leader and Bill for that of follower.

This illustration reveals a high degree of professionalism and for the vast majority of us this level of insight and confident interpretation lies at the end of training and experience. But anybody can begin today the long journey which leads in the end to this degree of competence. We can listen carefully to ourselves and others when we describe what happened in various groups to which we belong. Groups such as committees, the evening spent in a pub by friends, the railway journey with a few other people in the compartment or the coach tour through Europe. How far do those accounts operate at a superficial level and how far do they penetrate to the 'hidden agenda', to what is happening to those people in their relationships with each other and with the group?

For example, in terms of the illustration already used, two men might describe the same train journey from Birmingham to Euston in these terms:

1st Passenger   'The train left on time. There were four of us—two men and two women. At Coventry, a mother entered the compartment accompanied by her two children—a girl of seven and a boy of five. A railway official examined our tickets. We were ten minutes late in to Euston.'

2nd Passenger   'There were four of us in the compartment—two men and two women—all of us complete strangers to each other. We began the journey in isolation and in silence. We eyed each other apprehensively, wanting to make contact with a fellow human-being but afraid to make the first move for fear of being rebuffed or thought to be "pushing". However, when at Coventry, a mother entered the compartment with her two children—a girl of seven and a boy of five—the atmosphere changed very quickly. The children had no inhibitions about talking and soon we were

all listening to their prattle. One of the woman passengers produced some sweets. The young business executive in the corner
was prompted to talk about his own young children and in the end
produced photographs of them which were handed round amid
expressions of admiration. It was obvious that we were glad of the
opportunity of coming out of our shells and talking to each other.
When the ticket-collector had departed after his examination, one
passenger made a friendly remark about his attitude to us which
revealed that we had a sense of group identity. The time passed so
pleasantly that nobody grumbled because the train was ten minutes
late in Euston; in fact, none of us appeared to notice that we were
overdue.'

The view being put forward here (that training in group skill
begins by simply paying attention to group behaviour) can run
into two difficulties.

First, do not possibilities and progress here depend on character
or personality? We have several times used the word 'sensitivity'.
But certainly in part, we are here referring to a moral and spiritual
quality. Some of us are so egocentric, so wrapped up in our own
experience, that we simply do not notice what happens to others;
and if it is forced upon our attention, we do not particularly care
about what happens to others.

'Emotional maturity' can be described in terms of how real to
us other people's experiences are. Do we appreciate the effect of
our actions upon other people? Can we appreciate what is happening to them? Are we able to 'feel for them' or, to use another
common expression, to 'stand in their shoes'? Immature people
have simply not grown out of the necessary egocentricity of early
childhood when all external objects—even 'Mother'—are seen as
means to ends and never as ends in themselves. A modern novelist
described one of his characters as 'Edith, is a country which is
bounded on the North, South, East and West, by Edith'.

How can we say that training begins by simple observation when
the skill requires qualities which spring from the trainee's maturity? A few years ago, the writer visited a youth club and stayed
for one-and-a-half hours. During the whole of that time, a youth
of about sixteen years of age sat at a table in complete isolation;
nobody spoke to him and he spoke to nobody. There could have
been one of a dozen reasons. Was he unpopular with the rest? Or
did he find it difficult to make social contact? Had he quarrelled

earlier in the day with his father, his boss or his girlfriend? At last, unable to restrain my curiosity further, I asked the leader of the club, 'What's wrong with him?' Alas, she had not even noticed his long isolation; and subsequent events confirmed that she was not very sensitive to the needs of others.

However, that sensitivity is a requirement for group skill, is not an objection to the beginnings we have suggested; on the contrary, it is part of the argument. There are very few people who, training themselves to observe in the ways we have indicated, do not find themselves becoming more sympathetic people with a growing awareness of the feelings and needs of others. Or to put the matter another way—there can be no continuing and successful training in group skill which does not foster our own social and emotional development. In this subject we do not find that we gain a body of knowledge and acquire a set of techniques whilst leaving our own personality untouched. By the nature of the exercise, we are compelled to come to terms with ourselves—aspects of immaturity, weaknesses and prejudices within our own personality.

The following episode provided by Dr L. Button[3] is only one illustration from the field of training group workers which demonstrates that if we respond to the training, we ourselves become different people:

> Boris revealed that when he first took up a post as a full-time youth worker he was quite unable to conduct a conversation with the youngsters about anything intimate. He could now see that he set up all kinds of barriers so that it would not be necessary. . . . He was remarkably inarticulate about his feelings when struggling to convey this to us. . . . Responding to the obvious concern and sympathy of the rest of the tutorial group, he went on to tell us that the changes which had begun in his professional life had extended to his private life as well.

Long experience of working with groups of students on training courses for group skill, leads me to question whether anybody could sustain such a course and be the same person afterwards. But this should not frighten any intending student, since the changes largely consist of bringing into the light what has been in the dark corners of our personalities but still troubling us from there.

The second objection to the proposition we are putting forward —namely, that effective training begins by simply paying attention to group behaviour—is that it might on the contrary be thought to depend to a large degree on people's natural sympathies for others. Can it, in other words, be nurtured, if it has not been provided by nature? Are there not some people who seem so insensitive—we might even say 'socially-thick'—that they will never be good group workers, however much training they receive? Conversely, has not one to grant that there are people who spontaneously and actively display group skill—who take to the work as though they were born for it and that this can be so marked that training is not required and will effect no enhancement of their skill?

It must be conceded of course that we vary enormously in our native social skill. Just how much of this is congenital so that, say, the gifted have inherited for this purpose a suitable glandular system; and just how much of what appears to be natural skill arises from fortunate social experiences; on this issue the present writer has never been able to make up his mind. The practical point is that usually by the time people present themselves for training in group work, they represent within themselves various levels of attainment, though these are not rigidly fixed.

But this is surely not a fatal objection to the proposition. Perhaps it is permissible for me (in order to justify the statement) again to use an illustration from my teaching experience. As a subsidiary part of my job for eight years I have been working with successive generations of students in this subject on an in-service training course; they are nearly all of them older people, 'mature students'; no academic qualifications are needed for the course; the vast majority of them have lost the habit of disciplined study if ever they had it. These courses have brought me into contact with several hundred students. Reflecting upon this formidable experience, I realize that if the student is prepared to take the course seriously and to work hard, he would have to represent a quite incredible degree of neurotic and immature abnormality, not to make some progress; on the other hand, he would have to have an incredible level of social feeling and skill not, in the end, to gain something from a course which involves a large element of practical work as well as the study of theory.

So training begins in awareness and awareness begins in simply paying attention to group behaviour; in precisely the same way that for most of us, appreciating music begins by listening to music. But as in all these cases, we begin to notice the unsuspected; the drop of pondwater under the microscope is found to be full of life. We begin after a time to notice the hidden agenda of the group; what people are doing to each other; how they often speak to each other without using words; how they form subgroups within the main group; and a score of other realities which we shall notice before we are through. In one of his plays J. B. Priestley describes two possible sequences for the same group of people meeting on the same evening.[4] One is the conventional evening with the polite conversation which develops by evading a certain question and by refusing to recognize the hidden forces in their midst. The other sequence is when the question is answered and, as a result, what is really going on between these people is revealed. The hidden agenda is usually present though not always with the same dramatic possibilities.

A natural curiosity about other people is one of the few gifts which, to some degree, is essential for group understanding and skill; as P. L. Berger says,[5] 'the sociologist . . . is a person, intensively, endlessly, shamelessly, interested in the doings of men'; but this gift has, I think, been fairly widely distributed among the general population and most of us can rely upon it being there as a foundation on which to build an awareness of group behaviour that is more exact and disciplined and informed and that passes into understanding and skill.

So in the next section we give practical suggestions for using different group situations to increase one's insight. In general, I think it may be said that the reader will gain more from this book if he finds time to do these exercises. Of course, it is more fun and is more help, if two people undertake this homework, check up on each other and compare notes. Obviously, it is even more hopeful if we can study groups in a group. The following exercises lend themselves to both these possibilities. But they are also suitable for the solitary student.

Practical ways of increasing our understanding of group behaviour

In pursuance of our aim to be severely practical, the next section will be mainly concerned with simple group exercises.

Our own groups

This is the obvious point of departure. Tutorial experience constantly confirms that effective training in group skill starts from our own experience. Each one of us—the point has already been made before—belongs to several human groups. 'Family', 'friends' and 'work-mates' is a recurring though not exhaustive sequence. In each of these groups we shall behave differently. A policeman on duty will adopt attitudes which contrast with those which he may observe when he is romping with his children at home. A college gardener may be deferential in the presence of senior members of the administrative staff but authoritative when presiding over the local gardeners' association. A remote and aloof university don may be convivial on social occasions.

Strictly speaking, we may not say that we become different people in different groups. There remains a basic 'self', that is, if we are integrated personalities. It is tempting to say that the self remains in different situations, but our role changes: except that this is too sweeping since we all know that our occupational roles in particular are notoriously likely to affect our behaviour in non-occupational settings. Lecturers may be tempted sometimes to address their friends as though they were students sitting in the lecture theatre: policemen may be authoritarian in family affairs: some teachers, it is said, can easily be identified even when met as strangers on a holiday.

But with the sounding of these two cautionary notes, we affirm that in a certain sense we are different people in different groups, and to a great extent, we play different roles. More accurately, our behaviour will vary from one group to another primarily because we shall be trying to satisfy different personal needs in different groups: and second, because the expectations other people have of us will vary from one setting to another.

This brings us to the first exercise: look at yourself as objectively as possible in several group situations with which you are regularly involved. In what respect are you a 'different person', do you 'play different roles' and 'behave differently' in each? Why is this so?

Example[6]   Mrs Smith is a trained social worker, doing a full-time job, happily married with two children, now young adults—a boy aged sixteen and a girl aged fourteen.

Report   'I found this a most worthwhile exercise but not I believe for the reason you had in mind. I hope you are not too disappointed! I don't think I learned a lot about group behaviour. But I think I learned a lot about myself particularly in the family situation. I also realized that I was liable to carry the role behaviour that was right for one group setting into another group where it was not appropriate. All this I hope is made plain in what I have written.'

Family 'I began by asking myself how I saw my duty as a mother of teenage children. We are, I think, a reasonably happy family, though not of course without tension and conflict. I looked back on many conversations we had at meal-times and in the evening. My discovery was that I was inclined to be a bit too much of the social worker at home! By this I mean that there were several occasions when I was insisting that the children decide issues for themselves when they, whilst wanting to do just that, were seeking a bit of affectionate support. "You do like Jim don't you?" asked my daughter. "As a matter of fact I do", I replied, "but that isn't important. You must choose your own friends." This I found to be a pattern in our family group life.'

At work 'I confined my observations here to the group of colleagues rather than to any group of "clients" with whom I may be concerned. I brought to consciousness illustrations of what I already half-knew about us. We are good colleagues on the surface and, to some extent, below the surface too: but there are—mostly hidden—conflicts, tensions and insecurities among us. The boss, though friendly and easy-going, is seen as a threat by all of us: after all, he will have a large say in our promotion prospects. And I notice that none of us speak so openly in his presence about our professional difficulties and perplexities, as we do with the rest of our colleagues. We are a united group, feeling that we have to be since we are to an extent criticized from outside: and one norm is the standard set by professional social work. But some of our underlying divisions are revealed in the following two incidents which I recorded. At a casework conference, our least qualified member of staff reported on a client who was causing her much perplexity. Another member of staff, with a degree in sociology and professional training, offered a fairly detailed analysis of the case for the benefit of the unqualified worker, who thereupon became slightly confused and started an argument about experience counting for more than theories. On another occasion, I unwisely commented on a colleague's case which involved sexual behaviour: whereat one colleague, a spinster lady in her forties, commented sourly, "Of course, *you* will understand these things". And though she immediately apologized, I had caught a glimpse of another emotional river that runs under the surface of our group. The observation compelled me to see that we are ordinary human beings driven by the nature of our work sometimes to repress our true feelings, to be objective in the interests of the client and to make sure that our own emotional needs are not too prominent. Perhaps we should be a happier and more efficient group if we spent a bit more time together as human beings, just enjoying each other's company, admitting and accepting our deficiencies.'

At leisure 'A major contribution here is made by the social evening, entertaining friends to a meal in our house, going to the home of friends for an evening or spending an evening with friends in a pub. I tried to look at myself honestly in each of these three settings. I think I am reasonably good company, mainly because I like people and it is not difficult for me in this kind of group to fulfil the unspoken expectations of others which is to be accepted and appreciated. I don't want to talk shop and I have no boring political, religious and ideological line that I want to plug. Very occasionally—particularly with comparative strangers —I have found my professional role as a social worker a slight hindrance. It happens when somebody is talking fairly intimately about an experience or a perplexity, and suddenly, they catch sight of me, become aware of my job, and falter or finish lamely because they think I will be listening analytically. On most of these occasions, I am a bit cross that the barrier has been erected and I cannot be accepted in this setting just as a friendly human being. But once or twice, I have felt a slight glow of pride because my professional status was recognized.'

In the following example, a married woman student—seconded for training from a tutor's position—described in more detail her various family roles:

Daughter 'Emerging out of role as "baby" daughter who has to be controlled by parents as this role is filled by grandchildren. Tensions in relationship now focused on grandchildren and so parent/ daughter relationship is less intense. This is a transition stage during which I am preparing to take on the supporter's role as my parents age, thus reversing the relationship.'

Mother 'Children constantly manipulate my role to suit their ends while I constantly seek to influence their behaviour to suit mine. Constantly strive to bridge gap between ideal image of mother-figure and reality, e.g. I modify behaviour in presence of outside observers to conform more closely to ideal concept of mother figure.'

Wife 'Ambivalent attitude towards social role as wife—adopt subsidiary role in social groups where we are acknowledged as a "pair". But still seek means of establishing individual identity.'

Daughter-in-law 'Peripheral member of husband's large family. As the role of my parents-in-law develops as grandparents to my children my role within group becomes more secure. Ambiguous nature of role assignment characterized by lack of clearly accepted methods of addressing parents-in-law by name.'

Neighbour 'Relationships controlled by norms of group, e.g. rigid expectations about topics of conversation, time, mode and type of contents. Neighbourhood roles tend to be sex segregated— man contacting man and woman contacting woman.'

Tutor 'Adopt role of leader, information-giver and co-ordinator. Limit details of personal life which are revealed.'

Badminton Club member 'Newcomer to well-established group. Tendency for members to divide into smaller groups according to sex and age. I join appropriate group. Clear hierarchy established according to standard of play. I belong to lower status group and avoid social contact with those in higher groups.'

Looking at other groups as an observer

During the course of a normal week, many unplanned opportunities arise for us to look at and observe small groups to which we do not belong. Perhaps we arrive early for an appointment for a meal with a friend, and as we sit at a table waiting, our attention is caught by the behaviour of groups of people at nearby tables: or as we sit in the doctor's or dentist's waiting room for our turn, we notice the attitudes, actions and conversation of the other patients: or we are travelling home on the 'bus one afternoon, and at a certain stop, six rows of schoolboys embark and begin to lark about and tease each other: or whilst parking the car in the centre of the city, we sit in it for a few minutes and observe the human scene before departing on our business. Soon, having stepped outside the movement by being an observer—having frozen the picture—you become aware of different groups. Here are two couples standing and chatting on the edge of the pavement: they are friends who have met whilst shopping and they are exchanging news. After gazing into so many unfamiliar faces, they find it is good to meet somebody they know. And here is a small group of people who make a disciplined line: they are queueing for the bus. They are strangers who do not talk among themselves, yet they share a set of values since no one stands out of place.

The next set of exercises consists simply in using a few of these recurring occasions to make a more careful and disciplined scrutiny and observation of them. (If we find the occasions do not arise naturally in the next week, we can easily make them.) In each of these short observation sessions, the student is asked to isolate one feature of the group and to answer successively about three groups, the following two questions:

(a) What needs of at least some of the members were being satisfied here? Josephine Klein answers:[7]

> The expectation of satisfactions from group-membership derives to a large extent from the primacy of the family in the individual's experience. By being born into a family, he is shaped so as to seek out others for the satisfaction of his needs in many ways. Before he is aware of himself as a self-conscious being, while he is yet entirely dependent on others for the satisfaction of his material wants, he and others already depend on one another for the satisfaction of social and emotional needs. The need for interdependence will remain with him for the rest of his life: he will need to live his life in the context of small groups of others.

(b) What norms underlie the behaviour of the members of the second group? When a number of people have been together for any length of time, they have developed expectations of how each of them will behave to fulfil the purpose of the group and those who compose it. To quote George Homans:[8]

> A norm, then, is an idea in the minds of the members of a group, an idea that can be put in the form of a statement

specifying what the members or other men should do, ought to do, are expected to do, under given circumstances. One point must be made clear: our norms are ideas. They are not behaviour itself, but what people think behaviour ought to be.

Linton defines norms as a 'collection of rights and duties'.[9]

In the third exercise, the student is invited to look at a brief episode in the life of a group from the perspective of the leadership pattern which emerges. For the moment, the leader can be broadly defined as the one who influences most the behaviour of the others. C. A. Gibb comments:[10]

> Leadership exists for a group whenever its norms and structure allow the special abilities and resources of one member to be used in the interests of all. It is to groups rather than to individuals that the concept of leadership is applicable. The individual fulfils a role prescription and so provides leadership for a group.

So the objects of our scrutiny are need-satisfaction, norms and leadership—these three—but they call for two comments. First, that these things are happening: they are present to the observed as we shall see from the work of other students. There is more than meets the eye, because there is more than lies on the surface in the most casual encounter, say, between a few friends. There are unspoken laws governing their interaction, unavowed goals to be achieved, a concealed hierarchy to be acknowledged and a hidden agenda to be worked through. Second, we have been talking as though these three features—need-satisfaction, norms and leadership—represent different phases: which is patently not true: they occur with other phenomena, at the same time. Only in these exercises, after the fashion of social scientists and solely as a learning device, shall we isolate one of them and pretend that this alone is happening. So with each of the three groups observed we wear, so to speak, a different pair of tinted spectacles.

Examples of students' work

(a) *Need-satisfaction in the group*

Example 1 'Coming out of church last Sunday morning, I was in the queue which waits to encounter the minister at the door in that odd mixture of greeting, recognition, thanks and benediction. The Smithers' family were ahead of me—mother and father and three daughters, aged respectively nine, twelve and sixteen. In this setting it was a long session and seemed to last for all of five minutes, with the rest of us still waiting behind mustering our Christian meekness to conceal our impatience. Realizing that more time was being devoted to this encounter than was demanded by the conventions of the occasion—both sides seemed reluctant to break off—I fell to speculating on the satisfactions which were being gained. The Smithers appreciated being recognized and accepted by this leader, a public figure, who had just been exalted above a congregation to the whole of which his words had previously been addressed: to be accepted, greeted, enquired after, praised by God's representative, carried some of the symbolic overtones of being received by God Himself. The minister made sympathetic enquiries about each of the three girls in turn and on being informed, praised each one. A quick glance at the faces of the mother and father was sufficient to show how much this was to their liking: they basked happily in a reflected and possessive glory. The minister too went not without his emotional rewards. He felt he was fulfilling his role and their expectations in thus becoming more closely, personally and intimately involved with members of his flock. Moreover, he had just come from an occasion when his thoughts and utterances had been put before a whole congregation who had no acceptable means of showing their approval or disapproval of his performance. Small wonder then that he flushed with genuine pleasure when Mr Smithers convincingly assured him that it had been one of the best sermons he had listened to for a long time and a source of enlightenment and consecration not only to the Smithers' family.'

Example 2   'I arrived on the night before the day when I was due to hand in this recording and I had still not found a suitable setting for my observation. There was no time to think about it now as I was due at the annual college ball in an hour. And there it dropped into my lap like a gift from the gods: and I was so pleased and thrilled—fond as I am of these occasions—that I sat out a couple of dances to look round and confirm my revelation that here before me were people obviously gaining satisfaction and having their needs met in various group situations. The essence of the matter was the evident satisfaction it gave tutors and students to be with each other temporarily in this new role-relationship. In the classroom, the seminar and the tutorial, the lecturer must wear the mantle of a certain relationship: he must concentrate on particular aspects of the interaction and rigorously exclude others, such as, for example, the thought that this attractive girl-student is also a sex-object. But in necessarily adopting this professional attitude, the tutor must suffer some temporary loss of personality by suppression and also have a less than fully human relationship with the student. It is not surprising therefore that he turns with relief and satisfaction to those social occasions when in acceptable ways he can express other feelings for the student that have been previously sedulously disregarded. In a dance he holds the physically attractive female student in his arms and comes into close physical contact with her and no one will accuse him of acting unprofessionally. For the student, too, there is likely to be the happiness of the release of feelings that have been suppressed. However permissive the regime and democratic the tutor, he is still in term-time an authority figure, a threat, controlling the sanctions which govern one's behaviour, with the power to impose punishment or withhold rewards. The wish to develop an egalitarian relationship with him cannot normally have unrestricted sway. But now, for an evening at least, all that is changed. At the annual dance I realized that both staff and students were satisfying the need to express an aspect of their total relationship which normally had to be largely disregarded: it was something more than the mere change from a repetitious and boring routine: "a change is as good as a rest": for both parties it was clearly a release from a more inhibited relationship, the release of feelings which had to be disregarded, the satisfaction of the need to be accepted by each other at a different level.'

(b) Norms in group behaviour

Example 1 'Listening to the conversation of the schoolboys on the 91 'bus from town the other night, it seemed to me at first, that it was happily quite instinctive, really like the inconsequential play of puppies. Much of their talk was indeed of this nature. But after a time, I was compelled to admit—almost against my wishes—that there was at least one underlying norm which they all shared. It was compounded of their attitude to the school authorities, and their teachers in particular: they were seen as

3

"an enemy to be respected". The boys argued about many things in a light-hearted way: they discussed the merits of the two local football teams and various well-known pop stars and leading personalities among their fellow-pupils: strong differences and fierce loyalties were revealed in each of these areas. But when a member of the teaching staff was criticized, I remarked that nobody came to his defence. One boy in the group was criticized for being "Simpkins' pet", an accusation which drew an emotional denial. There was similarity in this group at one point: they accepted the norm that the teachers were "They" against "Us", and any member who forgot this norm was likely to be unpopular.'

Example 2 'Watched a 'bus queue as you suggested. Rush hour: 'buses full. About dozen people waiting. Strangers everyone: so it seemed. As they waited I could not see that any one of them spoke to any other. 'Bus came. Room only for five. In the excitement, young man at the back of the queue pushed aboard and secured a place out of turn. Shouts from the conductor to "hurry up" before he rang for departure. In the flurry, the queue-jumper "got away with it". As the 'bus sped away, the remnant of the group turned to talk to each other in indignation and commiseration. It was clear that this bunch of strangers—so aloof and distant a few seconds before—had all the time been strung together on the thread of an invisible norm—that queue-jumping was simply "not done" and anybody who breaks this rule is "not one of us".'

Example 3 'The best example I can think of is something that happened to me many years ago. I hope it is all right to use this kind of illustration. I went to live in a village and tried to revive a youth club which had a long record of violence and conflict in the community. We managed to get the club open again. But we had a lot of trouble. Nothing was safe. Billiard balls were deliberately thrown through windows. During the weekend, tiles were removed from the club building. I was in despair and on the point of giving up when something happened which slowly changed the situation. We were visited by a gang of hooligans from a neighbouring village: they destroyed some of our equipment and physically attacked me, as a result of which I needed six stitches in my hand. Well, the incident helped the members to discover that they had something in common. It disclosed and strengthened a norm. In the face of an outside threat, they realized it was their club and their leader who was being attacked. Club spirit was born that night: and gradually it became clear from that time on, that anybody who behaved in a way that would threaten the existence of the club should not expect to be popular with the rest.'

(c) *Leadership patterns*

Example 1 'I overheard five fourteen-year-old girls in the youth club discuss what they would do together the next night. Maisie was alone in wanting to go to the ice-rink. The others were equally divided between the cinema and coming to club. Yet in the end the decision was for the ice-rink. Why did Maisie get her way? She was clearly the dominating personality. She had more confidence and spoke more than the rest. She was the prettiest and the better dressed. She seemed to have the ability to help the group come to a decision when they were divided and her approval was most valued by the others.'

Example 2 'Chairman absent so secretary calls for a nomination from the floor. Eventually "A" put into chair simply because he did not refuse. In putting him in chair some were compelling A's participation: others probably wished to confirm his inability to lead. As meeting went on, three leaders emerged because they met various needs of the committee to cope with its tasks and problems. B was able to restore a relaxed atmosphere: C helped the group with its difficulties of communication: D was skilful in eliciting from the members their knowledge and views.'

Example 3 'My recording about leaders in a group arises from my attendance at a birthday party, held in her home for my niece who was then five years of age. There were six other girls present, all about the same age as Jane, except one girl, a neighbour's child, who was clearly two years older than any of the other guests. When the meal was finished, and the table cleared and they took to playing games, I noticed, not unexpectedly, that it was this older child whose suggestions for games and songs were almost invariably followed. Associated with her seniority were enhanced social confidence and knowledge: being older she was looked up to and envied by the younger girls: the group wanted to have a good exciting time and she helped this by providing information and forcing decisions.'

Two features are prominent in these samples of students' work. They are about 'ordinary happenings' and they are reported by 'ordinary people'. Here are two criteria of success for the tutor to use: first, that we discover that by looking at everyday events we can learn much about ourselves, about our friends, relations and colleagues, and about group behaviour. Second, that 'we'— who think about ourselves as 'non-academic, not very clever, not good at written work'—can write about them in a way that is often satisfying to ourselves and interesting for others to read. A recurring bonus on these courses is the frequency with which students discover that they have some literary powers of expression and enjoy describing in words various facets of the human scene as they see it.

Group behaviour illustrated from works of fiction

Authors are often 'psychologists before their time'. This ambiguous statement suggests only that novelists may intuitively anticipate the findings of subsequent psychological research. Charles Dickens (1812–70) anticipates in particular the theories of the Unconscious and some concerning aggressiveness that are found in the writings of Sigmund Freud (1856–1939). In the long story of man, the artist frequently goes before to prepare the way for the scientist: in fact it may often seem that the latter labels the parts of what the former has experienced as a whole.

Thus a reality is disclosed one of whose purposes can be to provide exercises for the student of group dynamics. For many story tellers—writing in an age before group behaviour was carefully studied or writing today but not familiar with the intellectual discipline—yet display an intuitive grasp of group behaviour simply because they have insight into and understanding of the human scene. And we can examine their stories from this point of view, whilst admitting that they were not written with this in mind and in all probability hold far more meaning than is revealed by our narrow specialism.

A good example is 'The flag of their country', one of the 'Stalky' tales by Rudyard Kipling.[11] Here the group is composed of a number of schoolboys who evince an unexpected enthusiasm for a volunteer cadet-corps—'Half of them were born within earshot o' the barracks' (p. 313). In a roundabout way, a jingoistic MP, Mr Raymond Martin, hears of this enterprise and secures an invitation to visit the school and address the boys: his subject is to be 'Patriotism'. His visit proves to be an unmitigated disaster that leads to the ruination of the cadet-corps.

Strictly from the point of view of group dynamics, what happened and what went wrong? The MP was an imposed leader who had no knowledge of and thus no respect for the norms and values which Stalky and Co. shared—'He had no knowledge of the school—its traditions or heritage. . . . But they would remember that they would not always be boys. They would grow up into men, because the boys of today made the men of tomorrow, and upon the men of tomorrow, the fair fame of their glorious native land depended' (pp. 319–20). Kipling continues:

> Now, the reserve of a boy is tenfold deeper than the reserve of a maid, she being made for one end only by blind Nature, but man for several. With a large and healthy hand, he [Mr Raymond Martin] tore down those veils, and trampled them under the well-intentioned feet of eloquence. In a raucous voice he cried aloud little matters, like the hope of Honour and the dream of Glory, that boys do not discuss even with their most intimate equals: cheerfully assuming that, till he spoke, they had never considered those possibilities. He pointed them to shining goals with fingers which smudged out all radiance on all horizons. He profaned the most secret places of their souls with outcries and gesticulations. . . . Their years forbade them even to shape their thoughts clearly to themselves. They felt savagely that they were being outraged by a fat man who considered marbles a game (p. 321).

The whole episode recounts, apart from Mr Raymond Martin, two other attempts at leadership from the headmaster and a prefect. Both are more successful leaders for the group mostly because their leadership is partly indigenous: they come from inside and grasp the values, goals and structure of the group. But what is interesting (showing a consistent pattern that one ventures to doubt was fully conscious in Kipling's mind) is that in the case of the MP, each leader attempts to communicate and lead non-verbally, with contrasted consequences (pp. 322–3):

After many words, he [Mr Raymond Martin] reached for the cloth-wrapped stick and thrust one hand in his bosom. This—this was the concrete symbol of their land—worthy of all honour and reverence! Let no boy look on this flag who did not purpose to worthily add to its imperishable lustre. He shook it before them—a large calico Union Jack, staring in all three colours, and waited for the thunder of applause that should crown his effort. They looked in silence. . . . The Head saved the situation by rising swiftly to propose a vote of thanks. . . . To this day we shall never know the rights of the case. The Head vows that he did no such thing: or that if he did it must have been something in his eye: but those who were present are persuaded that he winked, once, openly and solemnly, after the word 'enjoyable'. . . . The flag lay still unrolled on the desk. . . . The Head and the Commonroom, standing back on the dais, could not see the glaring offence, but a prefect left the line, rolled it up swiftly, and as swiftly tossed it into a glove-and-foil locker.

Perhaps enough has been made briefly of this one classic story to show the possibilities for the student of group work: close at hand lies a wealth of material not written for our purpose: and we only prostitute these works of art if we pretend that there is nothing more. But brief mention follows of other possibilities in fiction which the student is invited to work out in fuller detail for himself.

The Admirable Crichton is an amusing story from the pen of J. M. Barrie. It tells of how a high-class family is shipwrecked on an uninhabited island. Under the changed conditions of their situation, and in particular, under the necessity to stay alive, there is almost a complete reversal of roles. The butler Crichton now becomes the revered leader of the group since he has the skills necessary for their survival. When a ship is sighted off-shore that will take them back to civilization, the rest of the party want Critchton to continue his leadership role but he has too much sense for that: in the film version he appears on the beach ready to embark wearing his butler's clothes. Of course, one gratefully admits that Barrie's purpose was to interest and amuse, but the tale will lend itself to a heuristic function. It can be studied from the point of view of the changing values and goals of a group: the relationships which develop and the varied role structure: the communication system, including the conversations.[12]

Lord of the Flies by William Golding[13] is a rather horrible example since it shows how, under pressure, groups can be used for aggression and destruction and how the non-conforming individual may be destroyed. It is an ideal fictional setting for a group study since it shows what happens when a group of school-boys are stranded in a remote territory after an aircrash. Golding's story may be said to include a large emphatic comment on the fact that the group, under certain conditions, can be dysfunctional for the few as well as functional for the many.

Of course, there are films which can be used in the same way to increase our sensitivity, awareness and understanding of human behaviour in small groups. Again, it may be necessary to disavow this as a reason sufficient of itself to justify our visits to the cinema: anybody who becomes obsessed with one angle grows tiresome and boring. The intention is to add a dimension to our consciousness, not to replace all other dimensions. If this cautionary note sounds here superfluous, repetitive, even patronizing, its justification could be that I have known many students who would have saved themselves some unpleasantness had they heeded the warning. In all this work, we are describing what we believe to be valid categories but always with the qualification that life is more than any categories we can discern or invent.

But that in mind, one can look at a film like *The Dirty Dozen* through the microscope of our subject. In truth, it is not, through-out, a pleasant film, prone to delight in violence for its own sake. However, from our point of view, it tells the story of a group. All those who belong are criminals, already condemned, but given a last reprieve if they will 'volunteer' for an impossible attack upon an impregnable Nazi garrison—the time is the Second World War. Apart from the questions to be asked which we have listed at the end of this chapter, one should notice in particular how the leader establishes his position and also how the practices and skills which have put these men in gaol become acceptable and valued in another setting and with another goal.

Ryan's Daughter is a vastly different production, an altogether more memorable film in many ways. It comes into our category since attention is focused on a group (in this case the 'closed community' of the village) as well as on key characters. The central point for us is the working out of the conflict between an individual and the norms of the community. *The Go-between* is another recent film which readily lends itself to this kind of treatment.

Yet another possibility is to use episodes from one of the current television series. 'Coronation Street', for example, is not only a twice-weekly picture of Northern working-class life, it is also the history of a group with leaders and roles, norms and interaction. 'Softly, Softly. . . .' offers in particular an intriguing study of role-relationships in a highly-structured hierarchical system like the police force. How far up the ladder does one have to climb to be a relaxed drinking companion for Barlow? How much further to call him 'Charlie'? Are there any dizzy heights to be reached where one is permitted to slap him on the back?

The fact that these stories, films and 'soap-operas' were not produced primarily with the thought of our studies in mind is part of their appeal, freshness and charm. We can see that immediately if we now look at two examples of their opposites, that is stories that were written with the deliberate purpose of demonstrating an axiom of group dynamics. They are not without their value, but they are not so convincing . . . or so pleasant. We feel they are not 'real life'—and that is why they are not so convincing. The characters are stilted, artificial creatures, robots to prove a point, not living flesh . . . and that is why reading about them is not so pleasant or interesting.

Example 1   The explorers[14]

Situation   This group has been mapping and making geological investigations in a remote, partly jungle territory. They have got lost, have been attacked by hostile natives, have to guard against attacks by wild animals, and one of the party is injured so that movement is impeded. Their supplies are running down, and they have had to abandon their vehicles and some of their baggage. Their morale is good, and except for the injured man, they are in very good physical state.

Goals   All their efforts are now directed to getting themselves . . . to safety, and to preserve . . . the scientific records and samples they have collected.

Structure   They begin to discuss which direction they should take next. . . . This enables the group to come quickly to decisions on how to divide the performance of necessary tasks among members.

Group functions of maintenance and task achievement The group
had to strive consciously in order to survive in its environment.
The internal group relationships were strong. Each man was
aware of his dependence on the others and theirs on him. The
group's task had changed when they met their difficulties.

Example 2 A Welsh experiment

Howell Davies was born and brought up in a Welsh village, but
in his late teens he emigrated to the USA. There—a man of charm
and imagination, initiative and drive—he built a huge canning
firm and made a large fortune. But he never forgot his native
village. It was his lifelong regret that the place had never caught on
as a holiday resort, although it was situated near mountains and
rivers. In his later years the inspiration came to him to devote a
large part of his fortune to remedy this curious omission on the
part of the inhabitants of these islands. He initiated many schemes
to make his village known and liked, but only one of these concerns
us now.

Twenty-four young people, between the ages of sixteen and
eighteen, an equal number of boys and girls, were brought from
different parts of Britain to live in the village for six months.
They spent their time in visits of interest, climbing and attending
lectures on local history. Money was no object. A hostel was
created for their accommodation (later to find a more permanent
use). The young people were adequately compensated for their
loss of earnings during this period and a full staff was engaged.
It included a matron and a cook, catering and domestic officers.
It also included a teacher—one Septimus Hobblestick—who was
in charge of the project.

On a fine day in April, Septimus confronted twenty-four
teenagers none of whom knew each other and none of whom knew
him. He spent the next few hours learning everybody's Christian
name and the next few days trying to get to know them as people.
There was, as was only to be expected, a wide range of individual
variation amongst these youngsters of similar age. It extended to
ability, intelligence, social ease and confidence, emotional maturity
and physical features. At the end of a fortnight, Septimus had a
rough working-knowledge of the personalities of each member of
his family.

He knew, for example, that when Maisie wanted something, she must have it now, whereas Elsie could wait. ('The ability to delay response to stimuli is one sign of maturity'—he remembered the lecturer's phrase at college.) John could give a lead to the rest when it was needed, whereas Ernest shrank from responsibility. Bert was quiet, withdrawn and found it hard to make friends, whereas Ron seemed to proceed on the serene assumption that everybody liked him.

During the weeks that followed, the teacher learned much, from informal conversations, about the home and social backgrounds of his charges and he noticed that often their personalities were related to their background. (Another phrase from college training came back to him—'An individual repeats his primary group experiences in any other group to which he belongs'.) Mary had been spoilt at home and expected to be spoilt in the group. Dave seemed a bit neurotic, and found romantic relationships impossible—his father died when he was two and he had been brought up by a devoted widowed mother. Trevor seemed to have no standards—there had been little affection and less moral training in his home.

Of course, the group did not stand still. As these young people lived and played and studied together, many things were happening to the group as a whole and to individuals within the group. They developed their own code which included not boasting about the social position of one's family and not missing a turn at the chores. For most of the young people the experiment was an enlarging experience—they made new friends, gained new interests, and realized unsuspected possibilities about themselves in achievement and self-confidence. But not everybody was on equal terms of friendship with everybody else. There were popular heroes and heroines, one or two who were disliked by many and a few who made little impact on the whole. There were one or two close friendships and an example of *The Three Musketeers*.

Every night in his bedroom Septimus wrote notes on the events of the day and the developments of the group. He knew that his usefulness as a leader depended on his awareness of what was happening and he wished to put his observations down on paper before his impressions faded and he was left to rely upon his uncertain memory.

As time went on, he was also aware of the youngsters' attitude to himself. They had come to accept him as their leader and at different times they had different expectations of him—encourager, organizer, provider, facilitator. He fashioned his leadership in the light of their hopes as well as his own ideals.

Septimus was able to use his insight and skill to help the youngsters to gain from the experience and to move towards maturity. He learned who would be encouraged by responsibility, who needed praise, when to be active in introducing new ideas, activities and values and when to be passive and leave the group to work things out for themselves. He created situations in which individual members could profit by the wider experience of the whole group. In varying situations he functioned as they needed him. He worked with them to produce a fellowship in which 'the strong are proud to protect and not to attack or laugh at the weaker, in which the skilled are pleased to help and not be embarrassed about the exercise of their skill by ignorant rowdies . . . in which, in short, the members are protected from their own and each other's bad impulses and also to benefit from each other's presence.'[15] These desirable goals called for all the insight and skill of which Septimus Hobblestick was capable.

Professional casework material

In many areas of human endeavour, older and experienced operators accept a portion of responsibility for trainees and devise means to encourage them in their apprenticeship. Social workers fulfil their duty here partly by making available for trainees, their own professional files on the work they have done. These may be printed and made available to a wide public or they may be used in the personal contact between field worker and student. In both usages, of course, there should be proper respect for confidentiality.

Here then, close to hand, is another means by which the newcomer to the discipline can gain a 'feel' of the subject. So much is this the case that after a prolonged experience of assessing courses of training in group work, I would strongly urge that no student should ever be allowed to make his first attempts at recording until he has had the opportunity of a long and leisurely perusal of professional group work recordings.

It appears that the most economical use of time and space is to provide an illustration here and now in the text and then to provide a list of where other such useful exercises may be found.[16] In fact, the chosen illustration, taken from *Working with Youth Groups*,[17] cannot itself be quoted in full since it would take up too

much space and we content ourselves with an extract which
contains one episode only and the comment upon it:

> The art instructor had trouble with a boy called Pete, who
> never had settled down in the group or become interested in
> its pursuits. This evening Pete had been squirting paint at
> some of the girls, and the instructor asked that he should
> be excluded from the group.
>
> [*Comment*] The art instructor is good with those really
> interested in the activity for its own sake, and most of the
> members are getting a great deal from him. He cannot at
> present help Pete in the class because Pete is an obstruction
> to the progress of the other members. I must relieve him of
> Pete. I must try to see more of this instructor because he
> probably does not understand why we tolerate chaps like Pete
> in the club at all. Apart from Pete, the members of this
> group have progressed significantly in the last six months.
> They are seeing and appreciating things which they never
> noticed before. They have moved to where they are now
> because they were able to go to the art room together as a
> group of friends without having to commit themselves to
> using paint or modelling material unless and until they
> wanted to. The new interest which they now share has
> helped them in their social development too. The boys and
> the girls in the group now have something which they do
> together and talk about with absorption and enthusiasm
> whereas previously members of the opposite sex only made
> flirting or courtship relationships with each other, always in a
> self-conscious way.

Short this fragment may be, but the discerning reader will see
that it lends itself to the type of analysis that has already been
suggested.

(a) What is happening here? What does it mean for the different
participants? What can be done the better to forward the aims of
the association?
(b) What needs of participants are being met or not being met?
What norms are present? What is the nature of leadership?
(c) Situation: goals: structure.

Field research

There is yet another way for the newcomer to this country of groups to familiarize himself with its contours and make himself at home. This is by reading the research material of group dynamics. It is not nearly so dull or devastating a prospect as it sounds, containing—as the reader will quickly realize to his delight —much that is of sheer human interest: though this rash prophecy is far more likely to come true if we confine ourselves to the accounts of those researchers where the subject of the enquiry is close to what people would have been doing had the research not been mounted: in other words 'natural experiments' rather than 'field experiments'.

From a large constituency four examples have been chosen.[18] They may not claim necessarily to be the most important or influential of the pieces of work that have been done but the readability and interest of the written reports has been a decisive criterion of selection. In each case the circumstances of the research are briefly described and the line of research indicated. References in the notes facilitate quicker access to the sources for a larger and more satisfactory perusal.

1   *A Boston gang*[19]

William F. Whyte was a participant observer, himself living for several years in the neighbourhood of the gangs he investigated and openly accepted as a member of the gang which is the chief object of his study—'The Nortons' sometimes known as 'Doc's boys'. He shows that there is a clear role-structure and stratification: the position of importance on the hierarchical ladder is clearly marked for each and his behaviour defined. One of Whyte's most interesting discoveries is that one of the gang's most frequent activities—bowling—reflected not only the skill of the player but his social standing in the group. If a low-ranking member challenged a high-ranking player the rest used strong pressures —cheering, jeering and more subtle means—to make the low-ranker lose. Whyte is instructive in his exploration of the leadership of the gang—a crucial issue for him. Leaders are fair-minded, keep their word, work through the accepted hierarchy of authority. A leader spends money on his followers and acts for all at a time of crisis or when decisions are called for. The individual's capacity for getting on in the community is significantly affected by his standing in the group. Whyte's methods are also of interest for the reader. Notice his relationship to the gang as participant observer.

2   *Democracy demonstrated?*

The experiment by Lewin, White and Lippett is famous and much quoted.[20] The purpose of the exercise was to measure the effect on 'followers' of three types of leaders. Activity groups of five youngsters each were set up: the boys themselves were matched for such characteristics as physical energy, I.Q., popularity or leadership. They were set to work on model aeroplane building under the guidance of adults who had been carefully trained to operate in one of three ways:

(i) *Authoritarian* The leader here was strongly directive, assigning duties and roles, praising and blaming without reasons —'This is what you will do.'

(ii) *Democratic* Here the adult took an active part in the planning and completion of the work but as an enabler and facilitator, not a dictator. He left the boys free to work as they pleased and was objective in praise and criticism—'This is what I suggest you do today: what do you think?'

(iii) *Laissez-faire* This was a passive role. The adult here was not a facilitator, but rather a spectator. He did not attempt to control but offered a few suggestions. He tended to be aloof and uninvolved, though on hand to answer questions—'And what are you going to do today?' The field work consisted of watching the boys carefully to measure the effect on their behaviour of the differing and contrasted styles of leadership. (There was a concealed 'candid camera' which filmed some of the episodes.) Briefly, it was revealed that the varied modes of adult guidance produced significant shifts in individual and group behaviour.

(i) *Democratic* Work continued when leader absent. Relationships more personal and friendly. Individual freedom yet also more group-mindedness—'we-feeling'. Less tendency to find a scapegoat to blame when things went wrong. Higher productivity.

(ii) *Laissez-faire* Less achievement. Less ability for group decision and planning. Boys themselves likely to create a necessary pattern of leadership.

(iii) *Authoritarian* Evolved two marked patterns, aggressive and apathetic. More hostility, dependence, discontent and scapegoating: less group-mindedness, individuality and achievement.

3 Learning together

Ottaway (as we have already observed) has provided us with a useful account of what happens to a group of people who meet together regularly to study a subject.[21] The experiment grew out of an extra-mural course on human psychology organized by Leeds University. Though the advertisement made it clear that the methods to be employed were seminars rather than lectures, it was clear at the first meeting that the students who had enrolled came with the expectations that the tutor would give the information they required and facilitate their better understanding of human behaviour. They were disappointed to discover that the plan was for they themselves to provide, from their own experiences, the raw material for their progress in the subject. A few abandoned the course at this early stage, and those who remained were disappointed and passed through a defensive stage when they were reluctant to trust each other with their own experiences. But in the course of time, this was succeeded by what the author calls a period of orientation and a development situation in which, by pooling their own circumstances, they each gained better insight into the nature of human nature. On the way, Ottaway provides valuable suggestions about the best ways to work in groups and of the characteristics of good leadership: but the enduring contribution of the work is a practical demonstration of the reality that in many educational settings, a major part of the resources is the accumulated wisdom of the students and that this is very often more useful ven than the expert knowledge of the appointed leader.

4 Happy at their work

One of the most commonly-quoted examples of small group research took place in an industrial setting. The studies are known collectively as the 'Hawthorne' or the 'Western Electric Studies'.[22] In fostering the investigation, industrialists were motivated to learn what factors were conducive to the maintenance of a high rate of productivity in assembly-line processes, where the 'enemy' of boredom and fatigue was not so much a physiological condition, as lack of sustained interest.

In one of the experiments six girls engaged on assembling electrical relays, were put in a special observation room and subjected to various experimental changes. They were invited to work at a comfortable pace and on no account to make a race out of the test. The surprising result—contrary to management expectations—was that changes in variables like illumination had little effect on production levels which stayed high throughout. The conclusion is inevitable, and also instructive, for those who would understand group behaviour. The psychological conditions had improved and thus task-performance was higher. Being part of an experiment made the girls feel important. Even more influential was the interaction which developed by being part of a primary group: they became friends and developed team spirit.[23]

Conducting our own research into group behaviour

Those who are fortunate enough to be pursuing their studies in company with a few others have the opportunity of constructing a few simple projects which may bring home to them the 'reality of group' far more convincingly than any number of books, lectures or seminars. In the three suggestions that follow, six to ten participants are required:

(a) Form a ring, with, in the middle, in turn, one who with closed eyes gently rotates and keeps falling, relying completely on the group for support and rescue. Childish as this may appear it does in fact make real and vivid our dependence upon the group for support in various ways.

(b) Everybody writes on a piece of paper a question, dilemma or problem which is concerning them. All attempts are made to keep the result anonymous—writing with identical pencils, using block lettering, same size and type of paper. The folded sheets are handed-in to one member and then each takes one and without attempting to solve the problem or philosophize, says how they would feel if that was their particular problem. Anybody drawing their own, gives no indication but treats it as somebody else's contribution. The frequent result of this simple experiment is an access of group feeling.

(c) Engage in a 'morale-boosting' session. Each member of the group has an opportunity to say what he admires about the character and personality of other members. The result is that we learn how much the acceptance and approval of the group means to us and we often learn more about ourselves by remarking what, unexpectedly, is *not* said about us by others!

Learning through theories

The final suggestion for answering the question 'what is happening in groups?'—for helping us to find our way in what may be new territory—is only for the minority. But minorities are not to be neglected. We are thinking now of those who are stimulated by reading highly theoretical accounts of group dynamics, who are excited by conceptualization where authors have addressed themselves to general theories rather than to practical problems.

A newcomer of this class could do far worse than consider how Homans seeks to construct a universal system of behaviour in small groups.[24] To give only one example of his world-wide laws, he concludes that the more closely a man, in the activities he performs, realizes the norms of his group, the higher is his social ranking in the group.

But another approach is suggested here. As we wander bemused through the libraries of books on this subject, it may suddenly strike us that there have been a few key questions with which the theoreticians have concerned themselves. And we may come nearer to where we want to be, and find the going a little easier by concentrating on this or that subject, rather than on this or that author. The ensuing plan for this approach is governed by two considerations which seem proper to me.

First, do not give your heart wholly to any single theoretician. Inspect the goods carefully, even respectfully, but do not buy them. For us, the purpose of theory is not to provide the infallible truth or to write a new decree or to draw a blueprint, but to supply light on a practical situation with which we may be concerned.

Second, in what immediately follows, we give the merest outline of the matter, adding suggestions for further investigations. This is because the subject is too deeply embedded in the contents of future chapters to qualify for fuller treatment here. The three key concepts of theoretical thinking are:

1 *Cohesion* (Dictionary definition: sticking together, force with which molecules cohere: tendency to remain united). In our universe of discourse, we notice that small groups differ according to their solidarity, life–span, the sense of belonging of individual members, the degree of identification with the whole, the presence or absence of disruptive elements and morale. Theoreticians have

4

sought to describe universal extra-cultural factors which govern the cohesiveness of small groups.[25]

2 *Communication* Even the smallest social group over a period tends to develop a communication system which has features peculiar to itself: constituent elements are the forms of communication, their patterns and the relationship of communication to the stratification system. There are investigators who have achieved a massive concentration on the problem of communication in small groups.[26]

COMMUNICATION is also the influence of the group on the perceptions of individual members. A sociological dictum is that we receive a large part of our identity from the primary groups to which we belong. A major preoccupation of the theoreticians has been more precise descriptions of this reality. But not only is the individual largely the creation of the group to which he belongs, he may also react against it in terms of compensation, aggression, withdrawal, alternation or participation.[27] (Why does one son of a vicar become a monk and another an atheist?)

3 *Leadership*   In the past, there has been a concentration among theorists on the concept of leadership. Thinking about small groups has contributed to a 'revolution' where we no longer see the focus of leadership on the personality traits of the leader, but in the needs of the followers. Hence different types of leadership are identified appropriate to the situation. To walk down the paths which led to this conclusion can be an interesting journey.[28]

No attempt has been made in this whole section to give a complete and comprehensive account of the parts of the subject. It is designed to be a soupçon, an appetizer that prepares the way for the main dish. The section has been successful only if it has helped the reader to feel as though he was entering, with pleasurable anticipation, a land that is new to him. But henceforth our descriptions must be more systematic.

3 Observation

In the three chapters which follow we are admittedly putting asunder what life has joined together: though we shall claim that there is sense in this procedure.

The assumption on which we proceed is that the skill of a group worker is composed of three elements.

(a) *Observation* He sizes up the situation and understands what is happening here. From one point of view, as Homans has suggested, group leaders are people who simply see more of the total situation than followers. Homans comments:[1]

> The story of mankind is full of the unforeseen and unintended consequences of social action, and more often than not, they were unforeseen because the mutual relations of the elements were not understood. . . . A leader cannot examine the whole situation inside and outside his group unless he has a method for taking up each element of the situation in order and in its relation to the other elements. . . . What is needed is explicit, conscious, intellectual understanding.

(b) *Interpretation* It is not enough to see what is happening: we must go further and—though it is far more difficult—attempt to explain why the group and its members are behaving in this way. It is one thing to notice the 'delinquent' behaviour of a member of a group: but the observer may have taken an enormous stride if he understands, say, that the particular participant has chosen this course as a means of calling attention to himself.

(c) *Action* On the basis of the first two processes, the group worker may decide that he can take a course of action which will forward the aims of the group and its constituent members, although even here, the issue needs to be stated more carefully and accurately. A frequent decision for group workers is whether they should do anything or nothing: a masterly inactivity may well demonstrate the highest skill since if too much is done for the group they may neglect their own part. Successful and helpful leaders know when to be passive and when to be active.

Now it has already been conceded that this analysis is artificial. We have, so to speak, torn apart the flower of natural, living, spontaneous group behaviour and labelled the calyx, corolla, stamens and carpel: and in the process we have lost the beauty of the whole flower.

There are many people who have a deep-rooted suspicion that all analysis of human behaviour—all psychologizing—loses the essential feature. Studdert-Kennedy once put the issue in a bit of doggerel to which many respond with agreement. He describes the psychologist thus:

He takes the saints to pieces
And labels all the parts.
He tabulates the secrets
Of loyal loving hearts (*The Psychologist*).

Experienced people who do not want to escape into an academic dream-world will sense the danger and feel the sting of truth in the criticism. Yet analysis need not lead to remoteness: properly used it can contribute to appreciation of the whole. Modern psychology has trodden a tortuous path but it has led to a better understanding of human nature. Let us return to our analogy of the flowers. Wordsworth has pilloried the man for whom the flowers flash no message of beauty and joy.

A primrose by a river's brim
A yellow primrose was to him,
And it was nothing more (*Peter Bell*).

But the alternative is not a man who, in order to appreciate primroses, must eschew the study of botany: it can be that a deeper understanding of that subject will fire, not quench, his aesthetic passion. Similarly, we claim that our threefold categorization can enhance rather than destroy our appreciation of the wholeness of group behaviour. Still, the student should be warned against their artificiality and possible misuse. They easily give the impression that they are consecutive activities of the group worker. 'Now I am observing.' 'So I move on to interpretation.' 'At last comes action.' Usually, of course, they are concurrent, being simultaneous elements in a single attitude and act. The following illustration from a youth club session illustrates how all three—observation, interpretation and action—occur together.[2]

The leader noticed John standing at the coffee bar, looking disgruntled and handling cups and chairs roughly. The following conversation took place.

Leader   Having more trouble, John?

John   Yes.

Leader   The foreman at work again?

John   No (pause). Women!

Leader   Oh, I see. Bad luck. But don't take it out on the club equipment again this time, will you.

John   (putting down the cup). Sorry. (He was obviously unaware of what he was doing with the cup.)

Leader   Look, would you mind giving me a hand with a crate of squash behind the bar?

John   (Still in a bad mood) All right. (They go and move the crate.)

Leader   (while they are on the job). Try and take it easy, John. If you really like the girl, and if you want to, come and have a chat about it early tomorrow evening. I'll have plenty of time then.

This leader observed that there was something wrong with John: he made it his business to find the reason for John's upset: he arranged for John to help him and offered an appointment to talk over the problem.

Moreover, the three categories cannot, even in description, exist entirely separate from each other in water-tight compartments. This is at once obvious from the above paragraphs in which we have sought to portray each of them. In delineating observation we inevitably stray into the territory of interpretation: through all, we are also found to be talking about leadership which is the proper subject of the last chapter of this book.

Although it cannot be performed exactly, it is most useful to try to draw the boundaries between observation and interpretation since this is the area of most frequent overlap. In general it may be said:

(i) Observation is concerned primarily with the structure of the group and interpretation with its function: the first focuses on what we find in the group, the second on movements and developments.

(ii) Observation stresses the facts and interpretation the meaning of the facts.

Observation

(a) *Setting*

If we want to know what is happening inside any human group, we should begin by asking what is happening outside the group: its life will depend not only upon the interactions of the members, but on the pressures that come from without. And although, as Margaret Phillips[3] has argued, the informal processes can go far to modify the formal features, yet the latter should not be underestimated, as, it must be admitted, is the practice of many who write enthusiastically about small groups. None of them in fact— even the most casual and spontaneous—can be seen truly as an isolated unit hermetically sealed from the outside world.

(i) *Cultural factors*   Behaviour inside small groups will vary to a degree from one country to another since the participants will be affected by the norms and role-expectations of the culture they have imbibed. As we have already seen, the Lewin, White and Lippett experiments in varying styles of leadership suggested that the boys were happier, more co-operative, friendlier and more productive with democratic guidance. Perhaps one may be permitted to doubt whether the results would have been so emphatic had the experiments been conducted in a Communist country where obedience to the state is taught throughout the educational system.

A few years ago, I visited Hong Kong to conduct a course of training for social workers. At the first session, unexpectedly I ran up against two formidable Chinese cultural factors which effectively reduced my achievement. The group worker depends to an extent upon being able to judge what people are thinking by reading the expressions on their faces: here I was defeated by Chinese inscrutability. In like manner, he works to create an atmosphere in which members will become more and more open with each other and not see colleagues as a threat. Here the barrier was another Chinese cultural norm which impelled those social workers to save, not only their own faces, but mine as well. Though it looks a remote point of departure, yet we should observe first the cultural influences upon the small group. To take only one example, some of the forms of interaction will be culturally determined. If it is a coterie of actresses, we shall not be surprised to hear them addressing each other as 'darling': the same salutation amongst a committee of university dons would be at once more surprising and more significant. A German group are more likely to shake hands and Americans may establish social contact more quickly than their English counterparts. Observation begins by asking how much of the life of the group is affected by the fact that they are part of a larger world.

(ii) *Organizational setting*   There is a specific aspect of the cultural influence which lies closer to hand. Many of the groups we observe are a part of a wider organizational structure. A classroom is a part of the school: a staff meeting takes place in an establishment with clearly-defined hierarchical and goal structures: a discussion group is a part of a college, say. Briefly there are two features of the organization which are most likely to affect the life of the group. One is the total life-style of the organization and the other is the stratification system within it. It is common knowledge that organizations differ in their ethos and intentions. One may make a practice of seeking the opinions of everybody before a decision is made: the other may have a bureaucratic system which allows only a few people at the top to take decisions and that without consulting anybody on the lower rungs of the ladder. Again, one organization may be interested primarily in making a profit for shareholders, while another, like a hospital or a church, has a service function. The nature and variations of organizations has been a special study of sociologists.[4] We shall take here only one well-known work on this subject, whose insight lends itself to a demonstration of the argument that if we want to observe what is happening in a face-to-face group, we may have to look at the organization of which it is a part.

Burns and Stalker[5] described two contrasted work-organizations and used separate models for each. In the 'mechanistic' type of management, orders come down from above: there is a hierarchical structure of control, authority and communication and an insistence on obedience to superiors as a condition of membership. In the 'organic' management system, ideas are fed into the process from every level of the hierarchy: there is a network structure of control, authority and communication: commitment to the values of the organization is prized above thinking about the issues. The single point we are making is that the events which happen within a small group are likely to be affected by whether the total organization is 'mechanistic' or 'organic': the patterns of interacting in the overall structure may be repeated there, or they may be reversed. In a school where the head rules with an authoritarian rod of iron, discussion sessions may reflect the same kind of leadership, or by way of compensation, they may use another type of relationship with the teacher/leader to satisfy a need not met elsewhere in the school.[6]

As suggested above, a further aspect of the matter is that the stratification system (or 'pecking order') which marks the enveloping organization is likely to be reflected in the interaction process of the small group. Perhaps the Countess confides to her friends: 'I hope the members of the committee will forget my title and treat me like everybody else': but not surprisingly, one or two find this difficult. Again and again one has seen group processes ruined because the status of participants cannot be forgotten sometimes by the holders of the office but, more frequently, by the rest. Managing directors, headmasters and principals often persuade themselves that they are on equal terms with the rest, being treated as 'one of the boys', but usually this proves to be a comforting illusion. The deception may be revealed in the conversation, the bearing of the members or the different atmosphere which descends if the high-status member leaves the group. It is all perfectly natural and understandable. The high-status member usually has more sanctions at his command to affect our behaviour. He can impose punishments or withhold rewards—not supporting our promotion for example if he is the boss. (Perhaps it would be nice to say that the Countess is a friend of ours!)

In observing small groups, then, we need to look first beyond them to see how they are affected by pressures from the organization of which they are a part.

(iii) *Physical settings*   I recently spent a weekend in West London working on a course with a group of students. At the first session, I discovered that we were in the flight-path of planes leaving Heathrow Airport. Every few minutes the noise made it impossible for any of us to hear what the rest were saying. The experience and 'growing identity' of that group was seriously affected by an external physical fact. Sometimes one has seen people attempting to do group work with the members sitting not in a circle, but in serried ranks as in a school classroom, not realizing apparently that this arrangement is not conducive to sharing and will foster the notion rather that the one who stands at the front is the authority figure with all the required knowledge. A discussion group held in the corner of a vast cathedral may find that the setting is inappropriate to the intimate, friendly and relaxed atmosphere that is needed: the participants may even be found talking in hushed, reverential whispers!

Years ago, a headmistress took over a school where some of the pupils brought their lunch. They ate in silence, in a classroom, sitting at school desks, with a teacher at the front in charge. The new headmistress bought a gaily coloured cloth, set places at a table and turned a silent ritual into a family meal.

Physical settings are not unimportant for group maintenance, cohesion and achievement. The manager of a licensed discothèque in Manchester told me that in periods when attendances fell, he could, by closing a number of grilles, reduce the space and so, among the remaining customers, help to create the atmosphere he wanted.

(b) *Structure*

This object of scrutiny can be disposed of quickly: like the other sections in this area, it consists of focusing our attention on the obvious and reflecting upon the logic of common-sense.

What is intended becomes immediately clear by contrasting two group situations. The first is a committee. There is an official chairman and secretary: the whole procedure is carried on according to the constitution laid down for this committee or, if not, by an acceptance of the general rules which apply to committee procedure—participants address their remarks to the chair, proposals must be seconded before they can be discussed, voting on amendments take precedence over voting on proposals, and so on. We may well contrast this with a group situation where a few friends engage in a conversation in the bar of a public house. Now there are no appointed leaders, though for various reasons indigenous leaders will emerge to be recognized as the conversation proceeds, either, say, because they speak more than others, have more confidence, have higher general status or are better-informed on the subject, or for another obvious reason. Here there are no recognized procedures, no rule-book, no office-bearers. The ethos is easy-going and the behaviour of each single member is less defined: this group is less structured and more informal than the first. If one conversationalist forgets this and, say, attempts to 'pull rank' he will be deemed to have acted inappropriately by the rest: whereas in the first setting, a man who fails, say, 'to respect the chair' may be judged to have forgotten his manners.

There are many places where a stranger wandering in from outside cannot hope to grasp what is happening among a group of people until he has become familiar with the underlying structure, often unwritten and unspoken and taken-for-granted by all the regular participants: and the observer has to estimate both the degree and the nature of the structure. Suppose, now, an anthropologist from the Cotswolds is pursuing his researches in an Indian village. If he attends the local council meeting and listens to the debate, it is a fact that he would be unable to grasp what was going on without an appreciation of the structure, invisible to the newcomer but present to all the regular participants. Some members of the council have a recognized position because they belong to certain religious groups in the village: the total interaction process will be dominated by the notion of Dharma and Karma, which means that there is a duty for everybody in every situation and the destiny of all is ruled by fate.[7]

We should now concentrate attention upon a feature of the structure which has several times emerged in our general consideration, namely, role-allocation. Whether as the result of elections, appointments or neither of these, there will be clear expectations that different individuals in the group will perform specific roles that will have importance for the maintenance and/or the goal achievement of the whole. Past experience has shown that Ken is an 'encourager' and he will be cast for the part of 'morale-booster'. Tom has won a reputation for not giving up easily and finding answers in the face of impasse and the rest will look to him to be the 'facilitator' or 'gatekeeper'. Then there is Frank whose experience on the subject is acknowledged by all and is the 'information-giver'. Of course, these are only a few examples of the role-allocation which—formally or informally, by appointment, election or usefulness—is a prominent feature of the structure. And in asking the observer to be aware of this, we are telescoping a lengthy process since normally as a stranger one has to see the group at work for a long time before one can grasp the total role-allocation system in all its subtleties and nuances. Often when people come together in a new group, they are not entire strangers to each though the formation is fresh: obviously they will bring to the new association a history and pattern of previous relationships which will affect their interaction. Anybody who does not understand this reality may be at a loss to appreciate the behaviour of participants. He will not realize that in opposing A's comment B is expressing a long-standing dislike and that the pairing of C and D is predictable for anybody who knows them well.

'Structure' in this context relates to 'what you start with' in a group rather than what develops as you go along: and many associations of small numbers of people, informal as well as formal, appear to have a communication system or pattern which is the inheritance of the group rather than its earned income. In a northern industrial area, I was for a long time a member of many committees of voluntary organizations which brought together 'workers and bosses'. And though the former gave eager hospitality to working-class views, it was a fact that on any issue which was presented for our consideration, they were disposed to hold back until the 'bosses' had first expressed their views. Once again, it was a bit of the structure which was imposed upon them from without: in this case it came from the culture, the norms and folkways of the local industrial community of which they were a part.

It is Alex Bavelas[8] and his followers who have seen the crucial phenomenon of group life as consisting of communication. We may take for demonstration only two of his patterns of communication—the circle and the wheel. 'The circle, one extreme, is active, leaderless, unorganized, erratic, and yet is enjoyed by its members. The wheel, at the other extreme, is less active, has a distinct leader, is well and stably organized, is less erratic, and yet is unsatisfying to most of its members.' In the circle, participants commonly speak and listen to each other on equal terms: in the wheel, they communicate with each other through a leader, or hub.

Now it is true, of course, that Bavelas was writing about interaction: he built his patterns on what happened as he observed it in experimental groups. We are here giving a slight twist to Bavelas and affirming that it may be required of the observer to notice that the 'wheel' or the 'circle' pattern of communication may be built into the structure of the group even before interaction begins: and that where this is present, it is probably taken over from the wider cultural setting. The developing life of a group, as for an individual, relies both on nature and nurture, on inheritance and social experience.

Clearly we are concerned here with more than the *patterns* of communication: also inherited, and set in the structure to a marked degree, are the signs and symbols, the language of communication. Unless we have grasped these we shall not understand the facts that are conveyed by the messages in the group, and still less are we likely to grasp the meaning of what is conveyed. A man who wanders into an auction room not knowing the symbols of communication is likely to come away with unwanted goods. An elderly person listening to the banter that goes on between teenage boys and girls might suppose they are quarrelling whereas both sides may understand that a rude comment is a tentative romantic gesture. Reflection upon our common experience lends support. Most of us find ourselves, on one occasion at least, impelled into membership of a group which is strange to us and we are at a loss. I once undertook a long rail journey in the same compartment as a string quartet. They had an uproarious time, swapping musical jokes and making sly reference to the peccadilloes of members of the musical profession. But I was at a loss to understand much of the conversation I was compelled to hear: I was not familiar with the language. In most forms of human communication, it is the meaning and the intention which are far more important than the word, the phrase or the gesture. If a young man presents a young lady with a bunch of flowers, it is really true that 'it is the thought that counts'. Do the flowers confirm his love and plead his cause? Or are they really a friendly gesture because they 'parted forever' on the previous evening? Or are they flowers of condolence because the young lady's father has just died?

In seeking to understand what is happening among small groups, we are often required to distinguish the structure, the main features of which we have tried to identify.

(c) *Goals*

It is improbable that a human association will be formed unless there is a purpose to be served. Naturally, there will be variations in the emphasis and priority of the goal in the minds of constituent members: but there can be no cohesion without an overlap of purpose, implicit or explicit. Joe may be motivated to join the local branch of a political party primarily because he wants to meet the pretty girls who are members. Tom is more concerned about furthering the political intentions of the movement. But even Joe will recognize a commitment of the association to electoral triumph and will be careful not to show himself too blatantly opposed to it.

Useful observation, then, involves an assessment of the goals of groups. Here it has been common usage to remark that there are at least three types of goal-orientation:

(i) *Where the primary motive of the association—usually unrealized by the rank-and-file—is to satisfy a need of the leader* 'The tyrant is always stirring up some war or other in order that the people may require a leader' (Plato, *The Republic*). Twentieth-century inhabitants of the earth do not require this comment from ancient times to appreciate the reality: they are painfully conscious of the destructive examples in their times of political dictators who have provoked confrontation to make themselves indispensable. All such understand that more leadership is required by associations facing problems they cannot solve. In times of national crisis, the demand is usually heard for a 'leader' and demagogues have their finest hour and opportunity. As Jennings says: 'What makes this discussion of leadership so important is the growing, and perhaps tragic, loss of faith in the hero type. Ours is an age without heroes. It is questionable whether any society can avoid stagnation, if not disintegration, without them.'[9] At every level, leaders can be found who are self-orientated to the degree that they will work to make the group more ineffective if that is required and to make themselves more necessary: they will encourage over-dependence upon themselves rather than a process of self-determination in the whole and personal development of the participants.

(ii) *Task-related groups* Then we move to a distinction between groups which is found far more frequently in the literature of the subject. There are those forms of human association which from the beginning have a clear task in mind. It is widely appreciated that the achievement of this task alone justifies the activity. Failure here is total failure: if the objective is not secured, then attempts to console the vanquished on the grounds of valuable secondary gains, by-products, sound lame. In this context, the comments of R. L. Stevenson do not persuade:[10] 'To travel hopefully is a better thing than to arrive, and the true success is to labour. . . . For my part, I travel not to go anywhere, but to go. I travel for travel's sake. The great affair is to move.'

Once upon a time, there was a school football team which had a disastrous record: match after match was lost by a wide margin. The headmaster made a well-intentioned effort to console the members of the team and to raise their morale. At the school assembly, he addressed them in the presence of the whole company, and told them that success did not matter supremely, but that what mattered was whether they 'played the game' and enjoyed the effort. The effect was the opposite of what he planned and desired. The team lost more heart and made less effort. He had under-estimated the element of task relatedness of the team. At a subsequent assembly he modified his remarks and said that the success of the football team was important for the whole school.

In like vein, it would be inappropriate, and perhaps ill-received to offer the consolation, 'Never mind. You failed. But you had a lot of fun trying. And you made a lot of friends' to any of the following: a society to change the law about what they consider to be a social injustice; mothers on a housing estate who organize a petition to have a pedestrian crossing over a busy road near the local school; and workmen who take over a factory in an attempt to prevent it being closed down by the owners.

(iii) *Interaction-oriented groups* Conversely, there are those forms of human associations where the relationships which develop among the members are identified as primary objectives. Here Stevenson's comments make sense. For there is no precise end-product, no tangible criteria of success, no unmistakable achievements, victories or reforms, no measurable objectives.[11] Success lies among the intangible and imponderable realities of the process: that friendships have been formed, that members have learned to share experiences and have gained a sense of security and belonging.

Once again, of course, for a heuristic reason, we are pretending that the distinction between the three types is absolute and water-tight. Clearly this is not so. The most unselfish leader will be found, on closer examination, to be motivated partly by the need to satisfy his own emotional demands: and this is one reason why he initiates action. The most single-minded, dedicated and task-orientated group is composed of people who will display their need for friendship, acceptance and belonging. Their chance of success in the task will partly depend on the quality of personal relationships which evolve. Equally, the interaction-orientated group will usually be found to contain task elements.[12] Public houses organize trips for old people. Such groups often find that friendship is more likely to develop among those who share a common task.[13]

But though the distinction is rarely absolute, and it would be hard to imagine a group entirely compounded of only one of these features, yet it belongs to the office of the observer to estimate how the elements of each are mixed. As he looks at the group, he requires an answer to the question, 'What situation would truly constitute success for these people?'

Moreover, there is another vital facet. We have been talking—and necessarily so—as though the primary goal of a human association is forever fixed, eternal and immutable. In real life this is not so: there is a reality described by social psychologists as 'the displacement of goals'. In practice, a group may have a formal goal, written in the title-deeds, which has long been forgotten and overlaid in continuing experience. One notable feature of this is that there seems to be a gravitational pull in history for human societies to move from 'task-orientation' to 'interaction-orientation': as people grow older they become more concerned with maintenance and peripherally with achievement. They become less interested in the world and more interested in themselves, in the struggle for survival. Movements have their early days of 'the first fine careless rapture' and pass into a defensive stage. Religious movements begin with a message for the whole world but in the end become introverted, insular and devote most of their energies to the preservation of their organizations. A country can begin a Communist revolution that aims at spreading throughout the world but merely ends up with state-socialism.

And with small, face-to-face groups the observer must judge how far there has been a displacement of formal goals. He may find himself looking at a small society whose members think they are banded together to achieve a reform or a change in the law, but for whom the satisfactions of friendship in the association have long ago become paramount.

(d) *Tasks*

Behind the aims of the group lie specific tasks for the group. A committee, for example, usually passes through a sequence in which there is orientation to the subject, a collection of relevant facts, an airing of opinions based on the information and then decisions made when facts and opinions are brought together. A training group for social workers should consider the means which can be used in this situation to increase the sensitivity and skill of the trainees. What part respectively is to be played by lectures from an expert on the subject, pooling the experience of the trainees, creating opportunities for practical experience in the use of their growing insight and skill and the use of role-playing sessions? A drama class has to decide which work they will present involving play-reading sessions, choice of cast, planning the rehearsals, and fix the date of the production.

'What precise tasks confront this group, given their structure and goals?' is a proper, indeed a necessary, question, for the observer who wants above all else to know what is happening here. He may well be surprised by a recurring discovery: there is a prevailing tendency to identify ends more often than means: those who are clear about the goals of their intentions are liable not to give similar attention to the tasks which precede the achievement of the goals. Many discussions by action groups about social problems, for example, prove on examination to be an exploration of the ideal. This may leave the participants with an unjustified satisfaction that major objectives have been secured. But no progress has been made in planning precise tasks to be attempted that will bring the vision a little nearer reality. And reviewing the tasks leads inevitably to a consideration of the resources at our command.

More than the setting is to be observed

Throughout this section, we have been assuming that the main area to be observed is the total setting of the group—its place in the surrounding cultural system, its structure, goals and tasks. That attitude we believe to be justified. Before even the first word is spoken, the group has a reality; its whole life does not consist of, neither is it created by, the interaction that takes place within it: there is inheritance, original endowment to be counted, as well as experience: groups do not entirely make themselves: they are partly made by their social, cultural and psychological circumstances.

But the restriction of 'observation' to this specialism must not be pressed too far. In the active life of the group, there are events which come more appropriately under the heading of 'observation' than 'interpretation' since they have to do with facts rather than meaning. Though admittedly there is a rubber frontier between the two: some facts are only significant and may only be observed, because of the meaning we suspect them of containing. That Joe never speaks once during a two-hour debate is a fact that reveals itself to observation, but is only interesting if we begin to ask 'Why?' The rise and fall of attendance: the demand for a greater frequency of attendance: the resignation of members: all these are facts which in themselves are unrewarding unless they lead on to interpretation.

Not without significance in this connection is the most frequent criticism which a tutor has to offer of the first efforts at recording made by students. This is the failure to distinguish between fact and meaning, observation and interpretation, giving each their due place. In fact many such students confine themselves entirely to observation and never venture into the more demanding area of interpretation. I have marked recordings which have portrayed a most detailed account of what happened with no attempt to make what must be tentative attempts to describe the rationale of this behaviour in terms of the task, goals and setting of the whole and the needs of the separate participants. Other students go prancing into the field of interpretation but offer no solid account of events. Still more fail to distinguish the separatedness of and the links between observation and interpretation, facts and their meaning.

The sole purpose of the present digression is to stress that although on the approaches we are favouring the techniques of observation are primarily concerned with the total setting of the group, yet they are not confined to this area and continue into the period when we are seeking to mark what happens in the continuing life of the association. This judgment may gain clarity and plausibility by the confession of a personal failing in which I have several times caught myself out. It has happened when I have reached conclusions about why a group is developing in a certain way. Later on, when looking at my impressions, I discover that unconsciously I have gone on 'to cook the evidence'. In other words, I have detected within myself a tendency to notice only those events which confirm my conclusions. It is at this point that I remind myself that interpretation must not be allowed to overlay what we are calling 'observation'. I must ask what is happening and

5

try to get at the facts whether these accord with my conclusions or not.

Some observation exercises

There is not one right way to observe which can be used by every worker in every situation: what is appropriate depends in large measure on methods which any worker finds workable for him and factors which arise from the situation. Effective recording techniques are employed, not by those who slavishly copy an orthodox pattern, but by those who work out their style based on acceptable principles.

The following examples are from the work of students who were asked to concentrate their attention on the external factors affecting the inner life of a group: in each case they present what happens in a residential centre for child care.

Example 1 'This observation was made when a new member of staff joined an existing unit for disturbed adolescent boys in a residential setting. There were three sub-groups. The first two were composed of staff members, the "hawks" and the "doves", that is those who approached their task characterized by authoritarianism and a demand for stricter control and conversely those who had a more liberal attitude. The third group was composed of the twenty boys in the centre. Here then was a unit with one goal in common, an assessment and diagnostic programme which provided the framework in which to work. The unit was primarily task-orientated. It was however left to the appointed leader of the house unit to implant these objectives. . . . The leader took an authoritarian role: and conflict arose when a young male assistant was appointed. This was his first post in a residential community. He had preconceived concepts of how to work with these boys: his attitude could be described as a "permissive" one. He questioned existing rules and values and became a real threat to the house staff in general. . . . During this time, it was interesting to note that the unit staff who were previously not very cohesive, became united by this new situation.'

Example 2 'This takes place in a short-stay children's home situated in the middle of the local council flats in —. We were told that our home was not serving its purpose, therefore a meeting would be held to discuss our problems with people who were running similar establishments. They were to ask us how we dealt with this or that particular problem and to compare our method with theirs. . . . The meeting started with a full attendance. The Chairman (our leading official) said the reason for the meeting was that we couldn't control the big children in our care. . . . Normally our staff can talk and defend their actions. But now we were all silent. We looked at the matron, then at the deputy matron, but neither was ready to help us. We started talking after a few minutes, but that wasn't really like us. . . . After the out-siders had gone, we had a meeting of our own. The atmosphere was different and so was our behaviour. We were surprised at first. Then we realized that the presence of strangers, who had come to suggest improvements, threatened all of us greatly.'

Example 3 'Our primary task was to prepare and present to the other groups on the course a series of role-play situations which would illustrate various aspects of residential work which we regarded as important. The other three student groups were not aware of what our task was, neither were we aware of theirs. . . . This then was our brief to compose two or three role-plays and after three months present them to the whole group (38 in number). . . . Our information was scanty. None of the six of us had any previous knowledge of this type of production, its possible uses or aims within our respective residential settings. . . . Like every other group, ours contained emotional relationships of liking and disliking which were part of our raw material. . . . We also had a hierarchical structure within the group. . . . One member who attempted leadership suffered because the rest of us knew so little about her: being an unknown quantity she was rapidly identified by the rest as a threat.'

It seems apposite to use these recordings to make two points. Surely it is a fair comment to make that these students, at the beginning of their course, are already becoming aware of the 'inheritance' of the group with which they are involved—setting, structure, goals and tasks. Second, they demonstrate once again how impossible it is always to draw a firm dividing line between observation and interpretation, fact and meaning. In the art of observing, they are sometimes simultaneously interpreting: moreover, they only know what to observe within a framework of meaning.

The observation scheme

In a moment or two we shall be making definite suggestions for observation exercises, using a few of the 'classic' examples and borrowing a few systems with due acknowledgments. But first we give a possible use of our own scheme outlined above and we are the more bold to do this, because the reader will discover that many observation systems which are submitted to him are prone to concentrate on the inner and developing life of the group to the neglect of the 'social envelope' in which it is contained and by which it may be restricted. In other words, using our language, a common practice is to devote attention to the history and nurture of the group but to overlook its inheritance and nature. Or, to put the matter another way, there is a popular prejudice in favour of the psychology of the group rather than its sociology. The theoretical side of group dynamics is a branch of the subject of 'micro-sociology' to be distinguished from 'macro-sociology', which refers to the study of larger human units. In the history of sociology, there have generally been two traditions or approaches or attitudes. One is about 'man in Society' and the other is about 'Man in society'. The first underlines the contribution which is made by the individual to the building of a social construction. This approach is well-represented in the writings of Weber. The second concentrates attention on the constraints which a society exercises upon the individual member—a favourite theme, almost a signature tune, of Durkheim. In group dynamics, perhaps on account of their orientation to psychology, it is as though in one aspect of their work writers come down heavily on the side of 'Man in society' in the sense that they are disposed to give insufficient attention to the pressures which come upon the individual member from the original setting and structure of the group. Another way of putting a large part of this issue is to say that in observation we are concerned with both inter- and intra-group interaction and relationships and that so far in the literature of the subject, it is the former which has been more frequently passed over.

What may be noticed about the scheme which follows is that much of it might conceivably be written before the first gathering of the group, though this clearly presupposes that the observer knows a great deal about the life and circumstances of the participants beforehand. This is not to imply that even in our strictest use of the term 'observation' we intend that it must be 'preactivity', only that in our explication of the term, the process exists on a continuum between ante- and post-natal.

Table 1   *Sample observation sheet from the biennial meeting of social work tutors from different training courses**

Setting	Whole group	Sub-groups	Individuals	Myself as participant-observer
(a) Cultural factors	Professional ethos grown up around social work in this country	One course has a religious foundation	One tutor is known not to be as sympathetic as others to modern trends	As a woman I am expected in our culture not to take too aggressive a role
(b) Organizational setting	All belong to an organizational structure where the ethos is 'organic' rather than 'mechanistic' (cf. previous discussion, p. 47)	One course has a head who is notorious for authoritarian tendencies	One tutor, less qualified and experienced than the rest, feels slightly under threat	
(c) Physical situation	They meet in dilapidated premises which are likely to have a depressing effect. They sit round a huge 'conference table'	One group starts the discussion after a long and exhausting train journey	One tutor is suffering from a heavy cold	Arriving late I have to sit back a little from the table
(d) Structure	There is no firm hierarchical framework and the status of participants outside the group is not influential. An appointed chairman and secretary	The tutors of one group occupy adjacent chairs	One tutor, specialist in group dynamics, has authority in this realm	There is no recognized role for participant-observer so I have to disguise my activities

*The entries do not pretend to be comprehensive but are only examples.

Setting	Whole group	Sub-groups	Individuals	Myself as participant-observer
(e) Goals	Overt – to increase their understanding of the training process Covert – to make sure that one course is not getting too far ahead of the rest			
(f) Tasks	To collect information on the basis of which an important decision will be made	The host course is responsible for the catering arrangements	One tutor reads a prepared paper	

Table 1 shows a sample observation sheet from a meeting of social work tutors from various courses. The account is semi-documentary, based on fact but with a liberal infusion of fiction for demonstration purposes. There is a group of agencies in this country who are engaged in training students for a specialized branch of social work. They meet twice a year, taking it in turn to visit the centre where each course is located. They have several purposes: in-service training of themselves looms large since they feel they have a lot to learn from each other: it is necessary to formulate a common policy since there are negotiations to be pursued with authorities on behalf of the whole group: the assembling is a social occasion much appreciated by the tutors. But what is written in Table 1 does not represent accurately a single one of those occasions: most of the entries have been invented to construct a teaching device.

Most books on group work offer their own suggestions for observation. It is true, as we have already commented, that they are likely to be concerned with the movements of the group and neglect the setting and as one consequence to be more concerned with interpretation than observation. But we think they have a present value and perhaps the most useful service is to provide a detailed example of one and record references as to where others can be found. The following example is provided by Dr Leslie Button.[14]

Recording by a group worker
A prompt list

A *The main events*
    I The activity of the group. (a) group activity (b) individual action
    II Maintaining the group—organizing the activity and keeping the group going
        (a) Discussion of plans
            (i) of immediate concern
            (ii) plans for the future
        (b) Were decisions taken?
            (i) the problem
            (ii) who initiated?
            (iii) how did the discussion go and who took part?
            (iv) what decisions were taken and who decided?
        (c) What responsibility was exercised by which members of the group?
    III Development or changes in purposes, ambitions, and values of the group, including required or forbidden behaviour
    IV Relationship between the group and outside people
    V Environmental factors that are aiding or limiting the group

B *Relationships, role-taking and the discussion of relationships*
    I The emotional climate of the occasion (e.g. friendly, hostile, apathetic, lively, cohesive, supportive, discordant)
    II Who was present and any change in the members?
    III The pattern of interaction and the communication induced by the activity
    IV Were there any developments or changes in the control of the group?
    V Relationships
        (a) the structure of attractions and rejections
        (b) who initiates, who follows?
        (c) cliques and their relationships
        (d) any special roles, e.g. leader, clown, scapegoat, pacemaker, etc.
    VI Discussion of relationships within the group

C *Personal matters*
   I Significant items of communication, introspection, revelation and compassion
  II An assessment of the personal outlook, difficulties, needs change and growth of individual members of the group

D *The worker's position*
    I The attitudes of individual members to the group worker and the group worker's approach
   II The affairs of the group—level of dependence or autonomy
 III Contact with other workers or outside bodies
 IV Action required of the group workers
     (a) in respect of group activity
     (b) in support of individual members
     (c) in contact with other workers

Button's is a formidable, even daunting, list: it would, of course, be an unlikely and disastrous error to suppose that for every group there must be an entry in each section: the report sheet proves to be a document with four sections.

Group worker's report
Group and function .... Report by .... Date

The main events	Relationships, role-taking and discussion of relationships	Personal matters	The worker's position

None of the observation schemes described in this chapter is put forward as being the one and only possibility. There is no 'right' method of observation, only one that is appropriate to the worker and his circumstances. In training groups, the tutor seeks to encourage each student to develop his own method whilst encouraging him to test it rigorously for usefulness (as a basis for evaluating and action), practicability and comprehensiveness.

One source of stimulus, encouragement and inspiration is to read the accounts of experimental group work and fix one's enlarging gaze—not for the moment on the object of the enquiry and the results obtained—but on the methods used to observe.

Again, our space demands that we give a detailed account of one only such experiment and supply sources of further examples.

Reference has already been made in another context to William F. Whyte's well-known study *Street Corner Society*. Fortunately, he did not neglect to devote a major part of his report to a description of his methodology. In one section,[15] he describes in helpful detail how he set about tracing the group structure of the Cataldo gang. There were about fifty members with an average attendance of about thirty. He had an apartment overlooking the store-front club and through the venetian blinds could observe their meetings. But the angle of his vision was such that he could not see further than the middle of the club-room and to complete his observations he had to cross the street and join the men. When the activities were in full blast, he looked round to see who was with whom, who was playing cards, talking together or otherwise interacting. He tried to remember any reshuffling. 'I managed to make a few notes on trips to the men's room but most of the mapping was done from memory after I had gone home.' It soon became clear what were the major social groupings and what persons fluctuated between the two leadership structures that existed in the gang. After recording 106 groupings, he found that only forty of them contained members from both factions, and that only ten of these contained two or more members of each faction. Further analysis confirmed the reality of the two factions: by observing who initiated activity in groups of three or more, he identified a clear leadership structure.[16]

Close at hand for most of us is a ready-made opportunity for observation. A good proportion of the citizens of our democratic land serve on one or more committees, which is another way of saying that they belong to a group which meets for discussion and decision.[17]

There is first then a task-orientation. And often we can trace a time sequence through which a committee will pass to reach the decision which is the goal of their endeavour. In a brief statement, the chairman focuses their attention on the matter in hand and this is reinforced by the secretary's statements. To reach the goal, statements of various kinds will be made—seeking information, giving information, seeking opinions, giving opinions: then these first two kinds of statements may be brought together to express agreement, disagreement or a firm decision. 'If the facts and our opinions are such, then doesn't this follow?' Below we give a ridiculously telescoped and stilted committee sequence to illustrate this and to introduce the symbols for each contribution:

	Contribution	Meaning	Score symbol
Chairman	We must decide tonight whether to launch an appeal for funds	The fact is we are meeting to decide about the appeal	Inf. + because he is giving information
Secretary	We have postponed the decision for the last two meetings	The fact is, etc.	Inf. +
Jones	How much is our debt to the bank?	Will someone please supply the fact of the size of our debt?	Inf. − because Jones is asking for information
Smith	I think we are getting ourselves a bad name in this town by being so heavily in debt	He is giving an opinion—it is not an incontrovertible fact. We recognize the distinction by saying sometimes to a committee member 'That's only your opinion'	Vi + because he is giving a view
Brown	I don't agree. People think we must have been helping a lot of people if we are in debt. They are far more likely to help us if they know we need money	I disagree with the last view and put forward two opposing views of my own	Agr. − representing Vi + Vi + for two expressions of his own views
Robinson	What do the rest of you feel on this issue?	Will you please tell us your opinion?	Obviously Vi −
Kennett	I think there is something to be said for both approaches	I give my view	Obviously Vi +
Chairman	In view of the discussion I should like to propose that we make a definite decision at our next meeting	I make a proposition	Pro. + representing a proposition
All	Agreed		Agr. +

Thus far we have seven symbols which could be used to score the contributions which members can make to a committee discussion. The first batch are all task-related, that is they could be regarded as necessary contributions and stages towards the decision which is the known goal of the enterprise: they are all strictly

relevant for our purpose. But as we know—and perhaps to our cost
and chagrin—not everything that everybody says in a committee
is strictly relevant. Seriously, perhaps it would be unfortunate if
it were, since this would suggest a gathering of robots who had
forgotten they were human beings. In practice even the most
task-oriented committee has an infra-structure of personal relationships and a hidden agenda in addition to the formal list.
Because we are likely to be satisfying some of our emotional needs
in a committee, we need a new set of symbols to describe the more
expressive contributions.

Broadly speaking, there are two categories—positive and
negative. Bales gives a long list which includes the following:

Positive   Shows solidarity, raises other's status
           Shows tension release, jokes, laughs
           Shows acceptance, understands

Negative   Shows rejection, formality
           Shows tension, asks for help, withdraws
           Shows antagonism, deflates other's status

Josephine Klein has provided a shorthand version of the expressive contributions which being shorter is not so accurate a tool,
but one that can be used at greater speed.[18] The following examples
use her symbols.

	Contribution	*Meaning*	*Score symbol*
Kerr	By the way—Have your children recovered from the measles?	I interrupt our work to make a friendly enquiry about your family	Positive expression and/or friendliness, therefore = Expr. + F.
Saunders	If this goes on too long I shall miss my favourite television programme	I want to withdraw from this discussion since there is something more important I want to do	Negative expression of withdrawal, therefore = Expr. − W.
Anderson	We usually have a row when you come to committee meetings	I interrupt the procedures to express my personal dislike of you	Negative expression of hostility, therefore = Expr. − H.

Many students who have learned about this analysis have gone
on to use the scoring system at subsequent committee meetings:

they have usually found it a worthwhile exercise which they can recommend to others. But before we extol its usefulness, it is only fair to point out two difficulties of the technique.

(a) *The speed required*   People often speak quickly in a committee and follow each other in rapid succession. The recorder may find it hard to keep up. He can help himself by preparing a sheet beforehand with names in the left column and headings across the page for the varying type of contributions. He should leave plenty of space and not be afraid to waste paper. This canon does, however, clash with another, governing the concealment of the activity as far as possible from the others present, lest they grow self-conscious and the spontaneity of interaction be diminished.

More complicated patterns of observation are possible than the simple 'one-dimensional' scoring of statements, made by each member of the committee. For example, you may want to know 'who talks to whom' and undoubtedly this will sometimes provide a useful map of the communication system. (And it is a fact, as we know, that though by the formal rules all contributions should go 'through the chair', yet this is often forgotten and remarks are addressed to individuals.) What type of thing they say to each other might also inform us about the friendship or hostility structure of the group. Often another interesting exercise is to mark how often people say, 'I', 'we', 'you', or use an impersonal pronoun. Over a long enough sequence and with significant scores, it could be supposed that one who tends to an extensive use of 'I' in this setting is not very group-oriented: a high score in the personal pronouns suggests somebody who is personal in his total contribution to the meeting: a frequent use of 'we' is a sign of identification with the group: whilst the heavy reliance on the impersonal pronoun hints at the factually-minded.

All these variations can be valuable ways of observing at depth what is happening in this committee, but my experience is that they call for a group exercise in observation: most of us, I find, cannot juggle with all these balls in the air at the same time.

(b) *Ambiguity in scoring*   This is a more formidable obstacle, with two parts. First, there is the fact (illustrated in our example) that there may be more than one score for each contribution. When people speak in a committee, they often say more than one thing and sometimes in the same sentence. In scoring, a quick decision is taken as to just how many symbols are required. But second, there is a dilemma which is both more perplexing and recurring. What we are scoring is not what people say, but what they mean and what they will be understood by the others to mean. And here many ambiguities intrude as, for instance, between facts and opinions. The single word 'yes' in contrasting contexts may express agreement, friendship, hostility or be an invitation to another member to make a contribution: only the circumstances and perhaps the tone of voice will give us the clue, which may still be obscure.

It could well be asked: If these ambiguities persist, is the method 'scientific'? Not, of course, in the sense that the word is often used, although it could be claimed that it is still more than impressionistic. If the sequence to be measured is long enough, then the few ambiguities will affect the overall score of any individual less and less. This is demonstrated by the fact that students who independently observe and score the same committee sequence nearly always find at the end that there are significant correlations between their results.

This section has been about difficulties in the use of this method so perhaps it ends fittingly with another truth based on the experience of many students. If one persists bravely over these obstacles, ease and skill develop quickly, normally after the third or fourth effort. Then one should give it up as a general practice, be a good committee member and find that one's intuitive perceptions of the interaction process have been notably sharpened. For we would want to claim that at least for a limited period, the practice of these observation techniques can pay a dividend, and is more than a game we play with no end-product. In this chapter we have confined our attention to the observational role of the worker and seen this as a basis for the exercise of his skill. But it seems right at this point to break out of this restraint in order to demonstrate the usefulness of interaction process analysis in the three associated areas of observation, interpretation and action.

Observation

Given a sequence of sufficient length, we may uncover the role-structure of the committee at this meeting. And if the scores were fairly consistent through a whole series of meetings, our results might even go as far as to suggest what kind of a person the member

Table 2   The role-structure of the committee

Member	Relative high score	Role	Score sustained on many meetings
Mr Pickwick	Inf. +	The information-giver. Perhaps on the subject under review he is the expert	Is he 'Mr Know-all' whatever the subject under discussion?
Mr Tupman	Inf. − Vi −	The facilitator. His contributions encourage others to give their best to the discussion: his approach helps to develop the total resources of the group	Is he 'Mr Educator' whose consistent approach is to encourage others to realize their own resources?
Mr Snodgrass	Agr. + Agr. −	The co-ordinator. He brings facts and values and fuses them into conclusions and decision	Is he by temperament and frequent action 'Mr Fixer' or 'Mr Intermediary'?
Mr Winkle	Expr. + F.	The morale-booster. The first participant who scores significantly in the task-irrelevant expressive area. His contribution makes people feel good, increases their self-confidence, underlines their acceptance by the rest and confirms the desired self-image of the participant	Is he 'Mr Friend'— one who in all his relationships exhibits a sensitivity and social skill which increases other people's possibilities by encouragement and acceptance?
Mr Weller	Expr. − H. Expr. − W.	The disrupter. He also scores highly in the expressive area but by negative contributions. He may inhibit group feeling and individual self-confidence and maximize conflict— though equally his unhelpful contributions may strengthen solidarity in the mounting opposition he evokes	Is he 'Mr Wrecker'? Does he over a wide range of situations in which he is involved operate to destroy rather than to create, to hate rather than to love? Is he perhaps 'paranoiac' sensing persecution and opposition every-where? Or impelled to withdraw from situations because he cannot develop personal relation-ships with others?

is. Table 2 contrives to make the issue look simple and unambigu-
ous in order to demonstrate the point. This is a simplified version
of the role-structure of a committee which can be described by
marking the interaction within, and it is based on Klein's 'shorthand' version of Bales's longer, more complicated system.
Consequently the latter provides a more detailed list of role-
descriptions as seen in Table 3.

*Table 3   Kinds of behaviour to be found in groups: interaction categories
and common role-definitions*

1 *Shows solidarity:*	(F)	12 *Shows antagonism:*
Energizer		Recognition Seeker
Encourager		Playboy
Group feeling Expressor		Dominator
		Special Interest Pleader
2 *Shows tension release:*	(E)	11 *Shows tension:*
Harmonizer		Aggressor
Group feeling Expressor		Self-Confessor
		Help-Seeker
3 *Agrees:*	(D)	10 *Disagrees:*
Compromiser		Blocker
Follower		Rejector
4 *Gives suggestions:*	(C)	9 *Asks suggestions:*
Initiator-Contributor		Information Seeker
Information Giver		
Elaborator		
Procedural Technician		
Gate Keeper		
5 *Gives opinion:*	(B)	8 *Asks opinion:*
Opinion Giver		Opinion Seeker
Evaluator		
Standard Setter		
6 *Gives orientation:*	(A)	7 *Asks for orientation:*
Co-ordinator		Co-ordinator
Orientor		Orientator
Recorder		Recorder
Observer and Commentator		Observer and Commentator
		Member

(A) Problems of communication		1–3 Positive reactions
(B) Problems of evaluation		4–6 Attempted answers
(C) Problems of control		7–9 Questions
(D) Problems of decision		10–12 Negative reactions
(E) Problems of tension-reduction		
(F) Problems of reintegration		

Our hope is that it now appears that this constituent of awareness might help to give us a more specific and accurate answer to the question, 'What sort of a committee did you have tonight?' At least we should be able to go further than the common replies of 'We were just wasting our time' or 'The usual' or 'We got through a lot of business.'

Interpretation

Moving into the realm of interpretation, we may be able first to decide that in this circle individuals are trying to satisfy some of their emotional needs since, as we have already suggested, most of us are conditioned by our upbringing in the family to seek our acceptance and identity through social relationships. It may be possible to identify an incident or series of incidents in which members of the committee have sought to satisfy their own self-image ('I think the rest of you will agree with me when I say that I have been a consistent servant of this organization'); seek moral support ('Wouldn't you have done the same thing under the circumstances?'); acquire confidence ('I am grateful for your expression of thanks for my work which I assure you means a great deal to me at this time'); welcome status ('I accept the nomination'); gain a sense of belonging ('I have always been proud to belong to this association and feel that through our common endeavours many friendships have grown'); and to look for co-operation ('I have a proposition to put to the meeting').

One commentator has said that the individual under stress in a group situation is likely to grow over-dependent, become aggressive or progressively withdraw from the situation.[19] Thinking back on our membership of various committees, we may be able to recollect examples of all three. (We may detect instances of one or more of these reactions in our own behaviour. That could be for us an important bit of self-knowledge. The necessity for the group worker to know himself is a subject which will be dealt with later.)

Example 1 : overdependence   Miss Spinks comes under criticism at the church's youth council. To her intense embarrassment and confusion, the youth leader accuses her in a discussion of being old-fashioned and out of touch with the needs of young people today. Her response is to say, rather breathlessly, 'But I think the vicar shares my views' (and turning to the reverend gentleman) 'don't you?'

Example 2 : aggressiveness   In the business meeting of a voluntary organization, the full-time officer is gently chided for having spent money on equipment without proper authorization: he is firmly asked not to repeat this course of action. Instead of replying calmly, apologizing and explaining the circumstances under which this expenditure was made, he launches into a bitter and irrelevant tirade on the failure of the voluntary officers to support him in his work.

Example 3 : withdrawal   A working party has been set up to consider how funds may be raised for the building of a centre for a voluntary organization. Mr Hawes makes a long and enthusiastic speech in which he puts forward a scheme to which he has devoted a lot of thought. When he sits down, the chairman rather deflatingly says, 'That sounds a grand scheme. But I wonder if it is practical. What do the rest of you think?' Each succeeding contribution questions seriously the feasibility of Mr Hawes's plans. He, poor man, is piqued to have his favourite brain-child scorned: moreover, he is embarrassed and deflated by their poor opinion of his idea. He might have passed it off easily and graciously: 'Well, it was just an idea. I hope one of you can think of something better.' He might have proceeded to expound, explain and defend his proposal. Instead he said, 'Well, if that is all you think of my ideas, I shall not make any more suggestions.'[20]

We may also be able, on the basis of our observations, to judge what is happening to the committee as a whole in the twin areas of maintenance and achievement. Josephine Klein suggests:[21]

Orientation	Were members orientated to their task? Was there adequate problem definition? Procedural discussion?
Communication	Were there inhibitions upon the ability of any to be understood by all?
Expressive	Was the atmosphere as warm and friendly as the occasion demanded? Enough group-feeling? How was conflict and aggressiveness handled? What tension-relieving contributions were made?

Information	Was the information required both available and made available?
	Did opinions tend to swamp facts or masquerade as facts?
Views	Was there a sufficiently free exchange of views?
Co-ordination	Were there enough timely expressions of agreements, disagreements and proposals?
Control	Was there sufficient guidance from the chair, or from indigenous leadership, for successful working?

Throughout these questions we are determining whether the committee realized its potential in expressive and task terms, in maintenance and achievement. They all contribute to one large question, 'Where were the gaps—if any?' The application of those criteria usually leads to committee procedure becoming both more enjoyable and more efficient.

Possible judgments about particular committee meetings spring to mind immediately.

(a) *Too task-dominated*   For this occasion there were too few contributions in the positive expressive area (Expr. + F.). This can be unfortunate on two grounds. Members do not enjoy the experience as much as they might: the emotional needs they bring to the encounter are not satisfied. And this may have repercussions for the maintenance of the group: people will be less likely to attend meetings though they may not be aware of the reason. I know of at least one committee—composed of 'academics'— where the organizers are constantly grumbling at the sparse attendances and where I suspect the reason to be that the whole proceedings are conducted in an atmosphere that is altogether too cold and formal. Often, in the performance of the task, morale is paramount and morale can be directly related to the psychological atmosphere.

(b) *Too much negative feeling*   (Expr. −H. Expr. −W.) This may be so obvious that it needs no elaborate scoring system to identify. But what may not be acknowledged is that there are ways to be tried—with no guarantee of success—to work out conflict and to relieve tension.

(c) *Insufficient control and guidance*   This situation tends to be marked by an absence of orientating remarks, usually from the chair (Inf. +, 'The fact is we are here for this purpose'; 'The fact is we must move on to the next question if we are to finish by 9 o'clock'): and by an excess of expressive, and therefore, strictly speaking, task-irrelevant contributions.

(d) *Lack of information*   Many committees are bogged down because lacking the facts to form the basis of a decision, they are left only with the option of arguing with their opinions, values and prejudices.

(e) *Lack of views*   This occurs, say, when there are a few high-status people whose opinions are well known and treated with exaggerated respect or where the atmosphere is not relaxed enough for people to express their opinions as part of the raw material upon which decisions are based: different value systems need to be explored and talked through if integrated action is to follow.

(f) *Lack of co-ordinating contributions*   Facts and values have to be brought together in expressions of agreement (Agr. +), disagreement (Agr. −) or in concrete proposals. A scarcity of scores in this realm may suggest that the conversation is going round and round the subject with no proposals for marriage between information and opinions. This could be an aspect of category (c)—insufficient control and guidance.

(g) *Lack of facilitators*   This is indicated by a paucity of information-seeking (Inf. −) and view-seeking (Vi −) contributions. In extremity, it means that we have here not a group but a collection of individuals who want to give their own facts and opinions, unwilling to listen to and take account of what others have to say and lacking a facilitator who will encourage others to give what they have to give to the encounter. The score may also reveal that a few information-givers and opinion-expressers wish to dominate the whole event.

(h) *Failure of communication*   This feature is tested at several points. One is the reaction which a member of the group makes to a remark that is pointed in their direction. 'A' may offer a friendly morale-boosting comment to 'B' who interprets it as sarcasm, whether because of 'A's' reputation in this matter or 'B's' suspicious, paranoid disposition, no matter. Sometimes the experts on a subject will use technical jargon, with no attempt to explain to the uninitiated: the majority, uncomprehending, may remain silent not wishing to lower their status in the group by revealing their ignorance: but they are thus effectively barred from participation in the task.

Action

When in the present anticipatory mood, we move to consider what action might be taken by an observer who had remarked on one or more of the preceding situations, we are making the very obvious point that there may be occasions when he can fill in the gaps either by his own contribution, or by eliciting a contribution from another person who is present. This possibility should be described with caution. At the risk of being tiresomely repetitive, we say again that good leaders know when to be active and when to be passive. It would be unfortunate if the following list gave the impression that the worker's interventions will be frequent in this manner. If they were, two disastrous consequences could follow. The worker's popularity, acceptance and usefulness might diminish: he could acquire a reputation as 'Mr Knowall'. Not less serious—he would then often be found to be doing for the group what they should be doing for themselves. Such workers— and they are not unknown—are dysfunctional for the education process, even though they can on occasions help to a speedier decision.

The following items then are only illustrations under the previous headings of what could be appropriate given the right circumstances.

(a) Much can be accomplished by the worker to create a warmer, friendlier atmosphere. Encouraging remarks, enquiries about personal circumstances, sincerely-meant morale-boosting comments often change the atmosphere and create a chain reaction. Sensitive people are aware of this and can see the hidden emotional agenda behind even the most task-related committee. One common procedure is to arrive a little earlier than the time of the meeting to give a personal greeting to each: and to be prepared to stay around a little after the closure, if people 'want to talk'. I was once present at a London committee where a member had travelled from the Orkneys for the prime purpose of moving a resolution which was lost! I noticed with what care the chairman sought him out after the meeting, not to discuss the resolution, but to flash convincing signals of appreciation of his attendance.

(b) Possible interactions to work out conflict and to reduce harmful tensions arising from conflict are easily described. One familiar ploy—not invariably successful—is to make a joke to take down the temperature. The teasing remark can be status-raising as can be seen by the following:

> Joe has just encountered heavy weather because his aggressiveness has been publicly rebuked by a colleague: Joe is aggrieved, scowling, sulking.

> *Worker*   'Part of the trouble here I think is that Joe is such a doughty fighter, that all of us hesitate to enter the lists against him.' Joe may have been rehabilitated without his protesting colleague having been downgraded.

Elsewhere, it is appropriate to bring the deep differences into the open, stressing their intrinsic, factual content and diminishing their extrinsic, emotional content.

> *Worker*   'Well, we have two opposite points of view here. It seems to me there's a lot to be said on both sides. Personally, I find it hard to make up my mind. Let's try and list the advantages and disadvantages of both.'

(c) As the usual expectations are that the officials—chairman and secretary—carry a major responsibility for control and guidance, the worker, who may be neither, has to tread delicately and tactfully here. He can help to express in personal terms what one suspects is a confusion general throughout the group.

> *Worker*   'I am not quite clear about what we are supposed to be doing. Perhaps I missed an earlier point that you made about this, Mr Chairman.'

More direct interventions may be called for:

> *Worker*   'With respect, Mr Chairman, I think this discussion is slipping off the rails.'

(d) A tactful suggestion might be: 'Is it possible for us to reach a decision before we have more information? I propose we postpone the issue until our next meeting, meanwhile asking our secretary to circulate the facts on those issues where there are differences among us.'

Items (d), (e), (f) and (g) belong together since they may require the worker to elicit from others the information and views which he knows they have:

Worker   I'd like to hear what Joe thinks about this. His special position gives him information, that I, for one, do not feel I have.

Worker   I know Elsie has some interesting views on this subject. And she hasn't spoken yet. She was telling me about them last night and I found them fascinating.

Worker   We seem to be moving to that conclusion. How would that affect your position, Elspeth?

(h) In this area, the worker, without undue pretensions, may feel called upon by the situation to be 'Mr Interpreter', though he should seek an unobtrusive style. Perhaps a 'little cheating' is permissible on occasions: when technical language is being used which he understands quite well, but realizes, from a swift glance round the room that others do not—but nobody is asking for clarification—he may say, 'I wonder if Professor Mandarin would mind putting that in layman's language for the benefit of people like myself.' There are manifest interventions which can be made when expressive contributions are misinterpreted. 'I am sure Sam didn't intend what you thought.'

In these, and similar ways, without being too intense or appearing to be too intense, the observer/committee member may make a bigger contribution to the efficiency of the committee, an efficiency that is measured in terms both of maintenance and achievement.

As we are all the time concerned to demonstrate that the skill is within the reach of 'average' people, and not restricted to the reach of the specially-gifted, we include below extracts from the recording schedules of students in their first year. On the right of the page, there is the discussion which arose from this effort between student and tutor, the learning possibility and growth point, as it was seen by the tutor: although it is important to remember that the discussion arose from the whole recording and is not usually justified by the brief extract. The principle of choice is that they illustrate features of early recordings which keep cropping up.

Student	Extract	Discussion point
Maisie	'What is the policy of the administrators? How do they want the staff to react? Realizing that they have a rather "green" group going through their hands, is it their wish to let them go out on a limb? Is it only as a last resort that the superintendent appears before the children? Only at times when there is trouble and the "big bad wolf" is needed?'	'This is useful worthwhile recording—but you tend to give your conclusions rather than the evidence on which they are based. Why? Are your conclusions arising from your evidence or are you cooking the evidence? Or have you simply failed to record the incidents, though they justify your conclusions?'
Petula	'At the team meeting the housemother said she felt Ruth demanded too much affection from the children. Ruth replied that she was demonstrative by nature. The housemother said she felt Ruth was trying at work to fulfil needs which were not being fulfilled in her outside life. Rhoda quickly said that we all had our needs.'	'An awkward moment! The actual words used would have helped us to understand better what was happening here. Was this the best way to help Ruth to gain self-knowledge? If not, what words would have done? Is there any general principle about group work which arises for you from this incident?'
John	'It was finally decided that Ronnie would be suited to act as the guard to the Tree House and that the decision on Tony would be adjourned until the following day. Tony could not get out of the room fast enough.'	'You have an acute eye for the observation of events but you rarely say why you think these things happened and what needs of individuals were satisfied in these ways.'
Ernest	'The building instructor was a little tired of fighting, content with his own department and the maintenance of the school. At the staff meeting he needed stimulation from the headmaster to join in the debate. In the second part of the meeting he was concerned in particular with maintenance.'	'This is a recording of great promise and good quality—both factually and in evaluation. But what you do not make clear in your role-allocation at the end, is which of these judgments came from your recording of the interaction and which from your previous knowledge of the participants.'

Student	Extract	Discussion point
Yvonne	'Bob was a great nuisance during the games session spoiling everybody else's fun. But I knew he had just had a letter from home saying that his father had gone to prison again and Bob was working-off his upset on the others.'	'Throughout this work you show a marked ability to look at other people and to evaluate their behaviour. But you never attempt to look at your own behaviour and evaluate that!'

The observation of groups and group behaviour is not a game we play without any end-product other than the kind of satisfactions gained from, say, the successful completion of a crossword puzzle, although it is true that, certainly in the early stages, students feel the intellectual excitement of the exercise and are partly motivated thereby to continue. But for us the exercise has a purpose both in the expression and development of our skill. Observation is—as we have repeatedly shown—the 'ante-room' to interpretation: we try to see what is happening before we can attempt to say why it is happening, although it is necessary to stress once again that this does not mean the two acts are separate processes in a time sequence.

On the threshold of the section on interpretation, we end the concentration on observation by a few notes which aim to be a transposition from one key to the next.

All community workers face the task of discerning the needs of the people with whom they work: they usually work with three 'tools' which are all 'dangerous but inevitable'.[22]

First, they judge other people's needs by their own. The inevitability is that we can only understand other human beings because we ourselves are human beings, and any community worker who slips into the habit of thinking of himself as somehow essentially different from the 'client' is heading for frustration and failure. We, too, want acceptance, achievement and status: feel the pain of rejection: are liable to be threatened. All this is expressed in the meaningful phrase we may use to express sympathy: 'I know how you feel.' The world is made up of millions of individuals who are each psychologically unique, but who inhabit together vast territories of emotional need. If that were not so, social interaction and much that follows—society, marriage, friendship—would be impossible. But there is a danger in using this method of learning about needs: we may unjustifiably and prematurely project our own needs on to other people and interpret their experiences in the light of our own. A youth worker who suffered in childhood from a drunken father may know too quickly and unreflectively what is happening to a club member who suffers a like disability. Our general experiences as human beings, what we share with everybody else, can be safe guides: undue reliance upon our particular, individual experiences can not only reduce our effectiveness, but make us positively harmful. Judging other people's needs by our own is a necessary tool, but to be used with care and thought and with the objectivity that springs from self-knowledge.

Second, one way of discovering people's needs is to ask them. They are probably in the best position to know. The powerful drive in Britain towards a more open, participating society and the enthusiasm for community development processes, rests on the confident assumption that there are many occasions when the citizens themselves know what they want and that they should be involved in the decisions behind community programmes.[23] It is the same with individuals, of course: 'The heart knoweth his own bitterness' (Proverbs 14:10)—and its own joy and hopes. Few of us escape the melancholy duty of having at some time to offer comfort and consolation to the bereaved. And we learn, for example, that there is no blue-print for these occasions. True sympathy is a personal gift chosen with a single individual in mind. One man means what he says when he says that he would like to be left alone: another will meet healing in company. He alone knows. On the other hand, we cannot rely upon people always being able to tell us what their needs are: they may not be articulate about these or other matters; they may not know what their own deepest needs are and they will only know when somebody (presuming in a sense 'to know what is good for them') puts the provision within reach, with no compulsion to receive it; they may be unable to distinguish between their 'wants' (short-term, brief satisfactions) and needs (long-term, lasting satisfactions). Among the most impressive leaders are those who help others to discover what their deepest needs are, who read the word in the hearts of men rather than on their lips. In the Midlands, a few years ago, a young curate made contact with scores of 'Hell's Angels'. Through a long relationship, the discovery was made that what they wanted most of all were opportunities of adventurous service to deprived members of the community. No doubt they themselves were surprised by this disclosure and they certainly would not have thus defined their needs on the first day they met the curate.

Finally, we guess, and often rightly, that people have certain needs because they belong to particular social groups—mothers, teenagers, handicapped, immigrants and so on.[24] The point hardly requires explanation. The experience of each one of us is compacted not only of an element which comes from membership of the whole society, and another from our own individual experience, but because we belong to different sections of society— and several sections at the same time—for example, on the grounds of role, age, religion or race. We guess what is happening inside people and hence their needs, by the invisible labels they wear, and the prominence of the label in deciding their identity whether it be 'West Indian', 'Grandmother', 'prison warder', 'Roman Catholic', 'Protestant' or 'Jew'. And the provision of educational and social services in any country is tested by the ability to cater for every- body *and* for minority groups, to meet the needs of the people simply because they are members of the community, and to meet the needs which arise because each person belongs to a sub- group. Thus 'immigrants' in large areas have the same needs as everybody else: but they may also have special needs. The same holds for adolescents and it is significant that during recent years, in many parts of the country, 'Youth service' has become 'Youth and community service'.[25] The Plowden Report on primary education[26] extended the argument to the schooling of small children: 'If you give exactly the same to everybody, you deprive some because their needs are greater', was its message.

So this approach can help: but it, too, has limitations and pitfalls. There is a temptation to rush to conclusions about a man because we have identified his social group. This practice is common enough to have earned the title 'ethnocentric thinking', which identifies the tendency to understand people by, so to speak, putting them in boxes. Fortunately, individual men and women will not fit into neat categories: they obstinately insist upon being their unique selves: but our premature conclusions may preclude us from seeing them as they truly are: having 'summed them up' we shall find everything they do confirms our categoriza- tion: we have made about them a 'self-fulfilling' prophecy. But although this approach is capable of gross misuse, this does not mean we can dispense with it: some of the most notorious examples of insensitivity in our community arise precisely from our failure to give due weight to the impact of social group affiliations, as when, for example, we unthinkingly expect a Jamaican, who came to Britain when he was twenty-five years old, to know all 'the social ropes' as though he had been born and educated in Britain and had imbibed its culture; or when we expect to find teenagers with 'old heads on young shoulders'; or when official documents are written about social provisions which the semi-illiterate cannot read or, if they can read, cannot understand.

To these three familiar, everyday and traditional ways of trying to understand what is happening inside our neighbour, we have added a fourth, which is a little more self-conscious and deliberate, and, correspondingly, less intuitive and which calls for self-training. This is, of course, that by carefully observing the behaviour of others in small face-to-face groups we can sometimes gain a better knowledge of what their needs are, since—as we know from day-to-day experience—we all of us tend to express our inner feelings by our behaviour. A man who blushes is probably embarrassed; a woman who cries is probably sad; a child with tantrums probably feels frustrated. In the kind of observation that is considered here, we are merely carrying the normal procedures of interpreting human behaviour to a degree that seeks to be more exact, careful, objective and organized.

Of course, observing is a selective process: we cannot observe everything: we must have some principle of choice: and to that extent our observation is evaluative and interpretative. But it need not be less objective on that account. Scientists also look at a selection of facts in the light of their subject and hypothesis. Historians could not possibly record all the events of a decade: their choice shows that they consider some facts more important for their purpose than others. In neither case is the integrity and objectivity of scientist and historian called into question. Similarly, without 'cooking the evidence', and out of sheer necessity, the observer learns to recognize that some acts in the group are more socially significant than others, although—as we hope to show— he must always be on his guard against finding the facts to fit his previously-held interpretations.[27]

Interpretation

Although it has several times been made clear that the distinction between the two realities is not absolute, yet in general it may be said—that in our definitions—'observation' focuses attention on the 'initial capital' of the group, that is, what is there before the first meeting, whilst 'interpretation' looks more frequently to be the dynamics of the group, that is, what begins to happen from the first moment when the members assemble; and, further, that whereas, on the whole, 'observation' is concerned with facts, 'interpretation' looks for the 'meaning' behind the facts. In the three simple reports that follow, we may note the transition from observation to interpretation.

'John arrived at the party about 9.30 p.m.'
'John came in, looking a bit upset, and searched the faces of the others looking for somebody.'
'John came in at 9.30 p.m., looking upset, anxious to see if Maisie, his girlfriend, was there. They had had a quarrel last night. Is he feeling sad and sorry and does he want to make it up before Maisie is attracted to somebody else?'

Of course, interpretation is far more difficult than observation: in consequence, students in their first efforts at recording are likely to be more tentative in this realm: the least confident are liable to submit reams of the most meticulous reporting of words and actions with no attempt to design any interpretative structures. But that it can be done is evinced by the following extracts from the offering of a first-year student on a course of group training for residential child care officers. He is reporting on his experiences whilst on 'block placement' for practical work when he was assigned to a school attended by children in care. In the following extract, he concentrates on the roles that he thinks are played by different members basing his conclusions partly on an observational schedule which is not included here.

Tom is the scapegoat of the school staff. He stands for all that is old-fashioned and out-of-date. This role has been given to him and outwardly he accepts it and plays along with it. He is, however, not content with this role and would like

to change it but I feel he is too deeply entrenched to change
roles at this late stage. Ian does all he can to stimulate
and support new ventures but does not often bother to find
out and press for details. Malcolm tests everything . . . he
tries to make life easy for other members of staff and this
concern is often placed before his concern for the boys. He
does, however, often put himself out for the boys. John would
like to run the school single-handed but is far too insecure
when other staff are around. Frank is the comic of the school
placed in a role suited to him but a role he finds hard to take
at times. Donald feels obligated to stay on Tom's side. He is
well-qualified to run the place himself but would rather take
the lead from others.

The notion that an observer, without undue pretensions, can
interpret human behaviour—can say not merely, 'So-and-so did
this, that or the other', but also, 'I think this is why so-and-so
did this, or the other'—is based on a simple proposition, namely,
that 'All human behaviour has a reason', even if the reason
is not present in the consciousness of the performer. We may
think that this dogma is sometimes carried to doctrinaire extremes
as when, for example, Freud argues that even the most trivial act
of forgetfulness or absent-mindedness is unconsciously motivated.[1]
To actions which looked casual and accidental but had hidden
motivations, he gave the general name 'parapraxes'. Stumbling
indicated a wish to punish oneself, and leaving an umbrella
behind in a friend's house revealed that we felt obliged, or
secretly wished to return to it. 'Bungled actions, like other errors
are used to fulfil wishes which one ought to deny oneself. Here
the intention disguises itself as a lucky accident . . . a man may be
due, obviously against his will, to go by train to visit someone
near the town where he lives, and then at a junction when he has to
change, may by mistake get into a train that takes him back to
where he came from' (p. 82). Slips of the tongue may not be
accidental: they may reveal what we want. 'A young woman who
wore the breeches in her home, told me that her sick husband had
been to the doctor to ask what diet he ought to follow for his
health. The doctor, however, had said that a diet was not important. She added "He can eat and drink what *I* want"' (p. 84).
    We shall be unwise to hold forth too often about this motion
among our friends and on social occasions. 'I can see why you

find it difficult to remember the boss's name'; 'It is pretty clear to me why you had that dream.' Such remarks are unlikely to enhance our reputation as pleasant companions and they are calculated to kill the spontaneities of human relationships. Neither do they necessarily help people to modify their behaviour, since we are pointing to the symptoms rather than the cause. Thus, the statement to an inveterate nail-biter, that we appreciate that he does this not merely to keep his nails shorter, since there are more effective and hygienic ways of completing this operation, but that we guess he does it to express inner anxiety and tensions—such remarks, outside a very special friendship, may be rude, may break a relationship and are not usually designed to change the habit. One might almost as well say, 'Stop bleeding' or 'Stop having a temperature' since these events too are beyond his immediate conscious control.

But the insight—'all behaviour has a reason' even if it is an unconscious reason—is not destroyed by its misuse. It can further our understanding of others and shape our behaviour to them.

Some human behaviour is reflex action, but most of the rest is social action, that is, behaviour which relates to others. Hence the vast differences between two acts which from a physical point of view are very similar—a blink and a wink. Even the solitary Robinson Crusoe seems to have kept a diary which could be interpreted as a communication to an invisible audience. Indeed, there is a long and illuminating passage in Mead where he is arguing that the self is a 'social self' in the sense that we can treat our own personality as though it belongs to another person, hold conversations with ourselves, assess and reprove our own behaviour. And perhaps it is this possibility which most frequently lies behind the keeping of private diaries:[2]

> The individual comes to carry on a conversation of gestures with himself. He says something and that calls out a certain reply in himself which makes him change what he was going to say. One starts to say something, we will presume an unpleasant something, but when he starts to say it, he realizes it is cruel. The effect on himself, of what he is saying, checks him: there is here a conversation of gestures between the individual and himself.

As we move into an account of interpretative exercises, it could be useful to remind ourselves of the view that lies behind this section, namely that so much of our behaviour is social, affected that is by the presence of others, especially their immediate presence, as in the case of membership of small face-to-face groups. And we shall gain more from what follows if we have grasped what is involved here. For obvious though the point may be, it is a fact that most students are likely in their first efforts to concentrate a disproportionate amount of attention on the character traits of the actors and too little on the group pressures and their effects. Reading hundreds of 'first efforts' at recordings has persuaded me that there is an element in British culture which predisposes us to be better at casework than group work.[3]

Assessing a course of training for youth work in a college of education, I visited in the evening a centre where a number of the students were working. Among ten members present in the coffee bar, there were several intriguing group situations. For example, a few girls serving the drinks were obviously competing for the interest of a handsome male customer. Next day, in the interviews, I asked each of the students in turn to describe to me what had been happening the previous evening. Without exception, they provided good character studies of the one or two known to them. Nothing about group interaction. Yet all those students were undergoing a course in group dynamics.

In the following extract from a 'second effort'—brief but characteristic of the whole—only in the italicized phrase does the student move from individual orientation to group interpretation.

> Sara was thirteen, a tall thin girl ... on the verge of
> adolescence ... in the middle of her first girl boy love
> affair ... *this in itself placed her apart from the others.* ...
> Bobbie was twelve, fast becoming a lively Tomboy. ... James
> had a round face and wore glasses. ... Tina was a wild seven-
> year-old.

We have now made (as a prelude to interpretation) several points about the social nature of behaviour and perhaps they can be summarized as follows.

(1) The source of much of our behaviour can be traced to social pressures, to the remote or immediate presence of others, to our awareness of reference groups (those to which we belong or would

like to belong) and to general social pressures (for example, opinion polls reveal that our views are usually related to the social groups to which we belong).

(2) There are many human needs which can only be satisfied in association with our fellows. Argyle[4] gives a list of seven, indicating either responses sought from others, or types of relationships with others:

a. Non-social drives which can produce social interaction—such as need for food
b. Dependency
c. Affiliation
d. Dominance
e. Sex
f. Aggression
g. Self-esteem and ego-identity

(3) One frequent means by which these social drives express themselves is by our continuing membership in small groups. We join them and keep on belonging to them, not only to get something done and as an expression of efficiency but also to satisfy our needs, say, for dependence, dominance: for confirmation in the opinions of others of what we think of ourselves, confirmation of our self-image: or, maybe, to help us with our self-image, to facilitate our identity in our own eyes.

(4) In measuring the effect of the social environment on the behaviour of any one person, we literally do not know where to stop. Are we thinking about the part played in his attitude and acts by the region in which he lives? Or do we extend the sphere of influence to include the fact that he lives in a cultural entity called, say, 'Britain'? Perhaps we want to go on and say that his social environment includes the fact that he lives in, and to a degree identifies with, what is called 'the western world', as opposed to the 'Communist world'. 'Why did the waitress burst into tears?' we may ask.[5] The distressing outburst could be explored at several levels.

(a) She is a hysterical woman: she is tired at the end of a busy day when she has been 'rushed off her feet': she has just encountered a particularly difficult customer.

(b) In the restaurant she is part of a group, a network of workers, among whom tensions arise for various reasons at various times. Each person is under pressure: the chef not to waste food but to prepare meals quickly: the waitress is caught between the demands of the customer and the pressures of the kitchen staff. Moreover, for all there is the changing pace and intensity of work at different times of the day.

(c) There are influences upon the waitress from the wider society, emanating from the general culture (in this instance, 'the American way of life'). She is able to put pressure on the man at the counter in a society where women do not usually give orders to men. Some women are attracted to the job of a waitress in American society, because they believe it will be 'working with people' and —like air-hostesses—find that this aspect of the role is illusory.

An answer to the question 'Why did the waitress burst into tears?' can stretch the social environment to include the rest of mankind. Where do we call a halt? For we must. The answer for us is clear. We focus our attention on the influence of the small face-to-face group to which those we observe belong. We have, fortunately, a limited brief: we here seek the social explanations of the behaviour only in the small associations.[6]

(5) The last preliminary point is that we are searching not merely for the explanation of individual behaviour:[7] we are also concerned with the 'behaviour' of the group as a whole, and with sub-groups within the whole, for it seems almost at times as though these develop a life of their own.

In the process of interpreting any situation, we are confronted with many possibilities. It is unlikely that any two students will give exactly the same evaluation of the same scene. But I have been impressed by the frequency with which students under these circumstances will produce common areas of evaluation. And this is probably partly because not being able to assess everything, they look for the prominent facts and influences and use these as an interpretative key. We have seen previously how Whyte, working with Doc's gang, was for a long time puzzled by the hierarchical structure. And one day when he was watching the youths playing bowls it came to him like a flash, that the standing of each member was reflected by his performance at bowls—depending as it did on the amount of encouragement he received from the rest—and was in part created by his skill.

So we are looking for the big features of group behaviour, the central, not the peripheral, factors: and the recurring rather than the occasional. A tree may be bent in one direction by the prevailing wind although, when we look at it, the wind is blowing in the opposite direction. Since it is a practical, and not primarily

7

an academic exercise on which we are engaged, we cannot be comprehensive. But having found the interpretative key, we should not restrict ourselves to its use, saying: 'Whatever happens, I know that this and this alone will open the door to understanding': having constructed necessarily a 'theory', we must not so fall in love with it as to be blind to any contrary evidence which arises from the interactions.

In the suggestions which follow, a further artificial division has been made under different headings. Once again we have torn the seamless fabric. These realities are not separate and we observe them as occurring together: but they are separated for analysis.

Moreover, the various possibilities of interpretation are not exhaustive or systematic: but they claim to be more than random. They are areas of interpretation which, in the view of the writer, most frequently occur in life; and he is confirmed in this view because they are also the areas which earn most frequent reference in students' recordings. As we watch the movements in a group, we are concerned to ask what purpose is served by these changes, in terms of achievement (the task area) and maintenance (the expressive or 'feeling' area). As Cyril Smith says:[8]

> Knowledge of the way groups behave can be thought of as a kind of language. Without it the gestures of solidarity, the patterns of deference and esteem, the roles, are all meaningless but with it the social organization and dynamics of the group become explicable and predictable. The student must learn to master its alphabet; the signs which if they are grouped—into words—become indicative of group behaviour.

But the analogy of language only takes us so far since we cannot take statements at their face value: much depends on the context in which they are spoken and the demeanour and tone of the speaker. Neither can we give the same interpretation to the same event: silence, for example, can be as aggressive as abuse, or it may be as consenting as applause. Interpretation is a difficult, if rewarding, art and to be successful we need all the help we can gather from experience, reading and supervision. But we have to make a beginning and if we are always cautious and willing to learn, it is one of the things which is worth doing badly, rather than not at all.

The group as a whole

1 *Orientation to the agreed tasks and goals*

Sometimes a contribution is made under this heading by the chairman or secretary of a meeting in his opening remarks: 'We have a lot of unresolved issues to decide tonight': but it can also happen in less formal settings. A group of teenage friends are deciding how to spend the evening together and one is clowning. Says another, 'Don't lark about or we shall be too late to go anywhere.'

2 *Allocation of roles*

Even in small human associations there tends to be a division of labour. Again this may be on a formal level: 'Perhaps Mr Aldwinkle will be good enough to re-draft that paragraph for us in the light of our discussion': but equally it can be informal. As the conversation proceeds among strangers in the bar of a country pub, it becomes clear that one man is better informed politically than the rest. Henceforth his opinions are deferred to.

An analysis of role-differentiation was attempted by J. A. Davis[9] who studied 'Great Book' clubs in the USA. There was a marked tendency for the same person to perform the 'task-roles' of integrating the discussion elements and seeking clarification, whilst others performed the social roles—making tactful comments to heal wounded feelings, making jokes and so on.

3 *Leadership patterns*

For reasons mainly of their usefulness, some members of the group acquire more authority than others. During the early meetings, we may witness a struggle for power among those strongly motivated to dominance, but usually, in the end, a 'pecking order' is established. How people are listened to and how seriously their suggestions are treated usually gives a clear indication of the status system.

4 *Control*

Most groups develop norms of behaviour, which are a kind of miniature culture, a system of expectations of the ways in which members will behave. Anyone who fails to conform will be under pressure to do so, and, in serious cases, may risk rejection. In the Bank Wiring Experiment, as reported by Homans, there was a clear norm, an unwritten law, about the pace of work for each man in the team: 'If a man did turn out more than was proper, or if he worked too fast, he was exposed to merciless ridicule. He was called a "rate-buster" or a "speed-king", but at the same time a man who turned out too little was a "chiseler". He was cutting down the earnings of the group.'[10]

It is useful to identify at an early stage the dominant norms in the groups under our scrutiny, for they are the key to much else that happens. One frequent aspect of 'norm-breaking' is seen in the contributor who seeks to divert the whole from its agreed task and to tempt them to 'goal displacement'. He is likely to be rebuked by statements like 'But we are not here to discuss that', 'Can we come back to the point, Mr Chairman?' or 'And what has that to do with the matter?'

So to uphold the norms, a small association will be found to construct mechanisms of control. Mild punishments may be imposed upon the deviant or rewards withheld from him—as illustrated in the following extracts.

(a) 'F had often spoiled the friendly atmosphere which the rest seemed to desire. In later sessions I noticed that they were noticeably inattentive and fidgety when he spoke.'

(b) 'Not surprisingly, I could have forecast the results of the elections before the voting took place. Those appointed to office had shown themselves both friendly and strong supporters of the aims of the association: the deviants were all rejected.'

(c) 'After a time I noticed that "who-sat-with-whom" was some indication of popularity rating. There were many more chairs round the huge table than were required. Having arrived in the room, each member would take a quick look round and carefully choose his seat. The deviants were more likely than the rest to have vacant chairs on both sides of them.'

The mechanisms of control in a group vary in form, intensity and location. They may lie mainly in a strict formal code that applies to this association, or they may develop informally and slowly from the developing life of the group: they may be heavily sanctioned and limit the freedom of the individual: they may reside, say, in the tone of voice used by the chairman or the power to threaten held by a single member or a sub-group or the higher status of any based on position, age or experience. The mechanisms of control are usually highly individual to a group and the effective interpreter seeks to identify them early.

5 *The handling of conflict*

In the main there are three possibilities here. Conflict may be:

(a) Avoided because it is thought to be in essence bad. The seriousness of this evasive action is conditioned by the main purpose of the association. An attitude of 'let's avoid anything unpleasant' may be required in a social gathering but it can impede the process of decision and policy-making. 'Restrictive solution' is a term used by social psychologists to describe a situation where a group adopts a solution which is not in the best interests of its members in order to resolve internal conflicts.

(b) Allowed to disrupt the group and cause bitterness, resentment and hostility. This is when conflict gets out of hand. Handled immediately, differences can be used as the basis for better understanding, mutual tolerance, personal development and integrated action. Thus seen, conflict can be one of the most valuable assets of the association, but it can easily turn into a heavy liability. One way of putting the issue is to distinguish between intrinsic and extrinsic conflict. The first relates to the genuine differences that exist among the members—about facts and opinions, approaches and outlook. Extrinsic conflict refers to a common trend to allow emotional factors to prove an obstacle to agreement. This is when we judge statements not on their merits, but on personal feelings about who has made the statements; when, say, under the threat of being humiliated or defeated, we make wild statements which we afterwards regret; or we cling obstinately to our own highly individual use of words, even when they have been shown to be peculiar to ourselves.

> 'When I use a word', Humpty Dumpty said in a rather scornful tone, 'it means just what I choose it to mean— nothing more nor less.'
> 'The question is', said Alice, 'whether you can make words mean so many different things.'
> 'The question is', said Humpty Dumpty, 'which is to be master—that's all' (*Alice Through the Looking Glass*, chapter 6).

Usually, when conflict disrupts, it is because the extrinsic and emotional factors are allowed to dominate the scene: the issues become heavily personalized and are not treated objectively.

(c) Allowed to express itself but used as the basis for goal-attainment. Here, by contrast, the emphasis is placed on the intrinsic aspect of the conflict. A good discussion group leader, for example, will seek to bring the disputants back again and again to the real area of their differences. He will work to save them from being deafened by the emotional overtones of the contention.

The following illustration from a student's recording of a classroom situation illustrates the last two points of the mechanisms of control and the handling of conflict.

> The teacher's mildness of manner enabled one boy to turn the tables on him and call him by his surname only—as teachers often address their pupils in other schools. So there was a fair measure of the role of the therapist in this mildness of the teacher. However, the children often made it impossible for the teacher to assume a very mild role. They would often make crude references to his person. These coupled with an extremely high noise level, forced the teacher occasionally to become aggressive to the extent of pulling children about, shouting loudly at them and sending them to the principal or to bed. I am not saying that the teacher should not be mild-mannered or should be authoritative—what I am saying is that in these circumstances the teacher whose whole personality directed him towards a non-authoritarian role in the classroom was found occasionally by the group to make certain authoritarian gestures in order to keep control.

The first five areas of interpretative scrutiny—orientation to goals, allocation of roles, leadership patterns, control and conflict—focus attention on the tasks and achievement of the group. They have, of course, expressive undergirding, but the emphasis is on their primary feature. What follows are aspects of the association which have to do mainly with the maintenance of the group: here we are testing the psychological climate, which may, of course, have large implications for task performance. And part of our involvement is to gauge what emotional income is being gained by the participants as a whole.

The remaining features of the group as a whole have considerable areas of overlap, but they represent enough distinctions to be under separate headings.

6 *Solidarity*

To what extent does the group identify itself as different from other groups and, indeed, as different from the 'rest of the world'? Information on this score—as on all the other points in this section—comes to us through speech, gestures, facial expressions and actions large and small. Obviously, the more they have in common, the more they will feel that they belong to each other. Outside threats in particular will induce internal solidarity. Modern political dictators, for example, invent or exaggerate external dangers to encourage national unity. Similarly, small nonconformist groups in a cathedral city are likely to develop a commitment, an ability to weather crises, to possess an almost inexhaustible ability to live, a 'sticking-togetherness'—which is not always found elsewhere. Protestants in a country which is predominantly Roman Catholic will be more emphatically Protestant than their co-religionists in another country where they represent a majority of the population. Most writings on this branch of the subject use the word 'cohesion' rather than 'solidarity'.[11] It is possible to gain—in more precise detail than is our present concern—a quick overall view of some of the main writings based on research concerned with the subject.

From our more practical approach, we would rather ask, 'In which areas can we look for appropriate words, gestures, expressions or actions to tell us about the cohesiveness of the group?', or rather, since with most of us an approach from another direction is likely, 'When I say I think a group is cohesive, on what evidence do I base my judgment?'

(a) The strength of the internal relationships. For example, members of a committee who stay around to talk after the official closure of the meeting are likely, on the whole, to be more cohesive than those who leave immediately.

(b) The frequency with which people refer to the group as a whole (saying 'we' and so on) and the atmosphere with which this is greeted—receptive or rejecting.

(c) The regularity of attendance of the members.

(d) The willingness of individual members to volunteer for

duties, endure pain or frustration for the group or to speak well of the group.

(e) The friendships which develop through this association.

(f) The planning and sharing of common tasks.

(g) The relative elements in individual behaviour of co-operation and competition.

7 *Morale*

This is related to 'solidarity' but is not the same. It is possible for a number of people to be united by their common frustration, distress and sense of inferiority. Morale refers to the self-confidence with which they address themselves to their tasks. Success in action is almost always a powerful stimulus and failure in action discourages further attempts; although most leaders, conscious of the reality of morale, cannot always trace its causes. When morale is high interactions and suggestions flow freely. It is probably by observing these that we have the best chance of measuring the morale of the group by more than just guesswork.

8 *The forms of communication*

As we have seen, this is largely a 'given' element with which the interaction begins. But as time goes on there may be subtle changes in the verbal means of communicating but even more in the non-verbal. And this is part of our 'understanding of what is happening here'. A recent group which began with the chairman giving everybody an equal chance very soon passed into an era where it was dominated by one person. In the end—as each suggestion was made—the chairman looked at the dominator to see whether he shook his head in agreement. This is, perhaps, an extreme example: but more subtle changes in the instruments of communication are not uncommon.

9 *Patterns of communication*

In many groups that have a continuing existence, there are built-up, dominant patterns of communication for the means both verbal and non-verbal. Messages, both instrumental and expressive, will travel significantly down these channels. The observer may have in his hand an interpretative key if he is able to identify the dominant pattern of communication. This is, perhaps, best explained by describing an exercise with students on a course of group work training. I have found that this method stimulates a lot of interest. Moreover, it encourages students to use a group to which they belong to learn more about groups, to see that their 'laboratory' is close at hand. In this exercise, the whole class is divided into clusters of eight. They are each given a task which should be as close to their life-experiences as possible. It can be a problem-solving task arising from their work, which has previously been chosen for acceptability from other candidates for attention: it can be a project, the preparation of a programme for work or training: it can be more inward-looking in the sense that it is primarily concerned with an examination of their own attitudes, strengths and weaknesses.

Each squad knows that at an agreed time they will be required to present a report of their results to the whole class. But before they begin working together, they are told, 'You are asked to watch not only the results of your efforts, but *how* you work together. At the end, you will report not only on content, but on your co-operation. When the reports on your results have been received, another schedule will be handed round which invites you to record the way in which you have worked together. It is better probably not to know what it is now.'

So after the results are reported, the following document is handed to everybody, and sufficient time allowed for it to be thoughtfully considered and applied to their recent endeavours.

Communication systems groups

Most groups tend to develop a dominant communication pattern. The following self-explanatory models have been used to describe this fact. Thinking back on your recent exercise which of the following models comes closest to what happened in your group? And—most important—why?

The students make an active response to this self-assessment. Suddenly it appears as though everybody wants to speak at once. They have experienced the development of dominant communication systems which in most cases is far more measurable than reading about the reality in a book or hearing about it in a lecture. But it is when they address themselves to the question

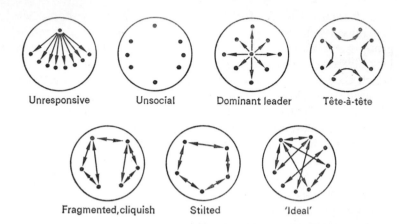

Unresponsive   Unsocial   Dominant leader   Tête-à-tête

Fragmented,cliquish   Stilted   'Ideal'

'Why?' that they move into an area full at once both of promise and danger: they are traversing a minefield beyond which lies victory, for the answer to 'Why?' may be the disclosure of facts about themselves—as a whole group, as sub-groups, as individuals —which are unacceptable and even unpleasant. In this setting, the skill of the tutor is often severely tested in helping the group and sub-groups to accept truths about themselves and progress through self-knowledge: in directing conflict into positive channels: in facilitating necessary protection for individuals from humiliation, from the loss of too much face and even from rejection.

Sub-groups within the whole

As a former employee, Antony Jay recently wrote a book submitting the administration of the BBC to careful analysis.[12] His main conclusion was that 'hunting packs' developed around particular projects or programmes; that these packs organized themselves to be physically close to each other; and that the packs were both relatively isolated from each other, but were also in competition.

In very much smaller human associations, we are familiar with the phenomenon of 'groups within the group' and the work of interpretation extends, not merely to recognizing these, but also to appreciating the reasons for their existence.

Sometimes this is easy and obvious: the conclusions commonplace, as in the following extract from a student's recording in a remand home.

There were two children a brother and a sister, the youngest
in the unit who felt the absence of the houseparents most of
all. . . . They had become more dependent than the others on the
unit because of their unsettled home background. It was
obvious that being together was the only concrete continuing
experience or relationship. During the day they would fight and
argue but at night getting ready for bed, they delighted to have
a bath or a shower together, laughing, hugging and kissing one
another.

Clearly, many of the constellations which form inside the whole,
are based on the emotional needs of the participants. (Nevertheless, it is a mistake to assume that the formations will therefore
be static: at the next meeting it can be that a shake of the kaleido-
scope has given us another pattern of human associations.)

Sociometry is a technique which seeks to measure the interpersonal structure of a group based on choices of association (it is
also a technique for basing leadership action on the results). A
simple exercise arises at a children's party. Four captains are
elected by the adult organizer and they have in turn to choose the
rest for their team in a game about to be played. Everybody
realizes that the choice will be on the basis of friendship as well as
skill. Some of the children excitedly cry 'Choose me! Choose me!'
There may be a sense of rejection among those who are last to be
chosen.

Operations like these tell us much about the standing of
individuals: but more sophisticated operations may tell us about
the patterns of relationship and hence the sub-groupings of the
whole. In Moreno's original experiment, 600 girls in a detention
centre could choose five girls with whom they wished to share a
dormitory: then five girls with whom they would least like to share a
dormitory. These fuller surveys can reveal the clusters of acceptance and rejection: how integrated and close-knit the group is:
whether, say, it is composed of two factions or a number of
cliques.

Without indulging these elaborate procedures, are there any
ways in which we can recognize the friendship patterns? Of course
there are, and many of them we are using already, perhaps
intuitively and without being fully aware of what we are doing.
In a group that meets regularly there are almost always areas
where people display their personal preferences. Sub-groups tend

to keep together physically, to interact more frequently than with others and to support each other. The first point both tutor and student have found most revealing. Watch a man enter a room where many others are present—a commonroom, a ballroom—and notice how carefully he chooses which knot of humans he joins. And if it is a daily occurrence, like entering the staff commonroom for mid-morning coffee, notice how often he will make the same choice. A tutor cannot help noticing how in a weekly seminar, the students will sit week after week in the same place, near to the same place and near to the same companions. They are not merely creatures of habit: they are expressing choices.

The significance of divisions within the whole goes beyond the expression of friendship and the search for emotional support. Obviously, it can represent a cluster of interests. A staff-student council in an academic establishment, for example, will show a polarization of staff and students on any major issue.

The fact of sub-groupings may be good or bad (for the achievement of goals or for the personal development of the individuals) depending upon the circumstances. Under either of these headings the causes of partition may be tested for the following constituents —apart from reasons of friendship which we have already noticed:

(a) The group is too large for personal face-to-face satisfactions;
(b) The sub-groups represent minority interests which are not felt to be reflected in the whole;
(c) The sub-groups represent needs which are not felt to be catered for;
(d) Individuals have developed to the point where they no longer need the group in quite the same way: 'Tom and Mary used to come to the youth club every night it was open: now they are courting, we only see them once a week';
(e) A sub-group represents those who are less committed and have become less ethnocentric.

The individuals in the group

George McCall and J. Simmons:[13]

> Man, both as animal and as dreamer, is highly dependent upon interaction with his fellows. His daily life, which takes place in the intersection of these two worlds, must be lived in consort

with the other humans on the scene. . . . Identity, like freedom,
must be won and re-won every day. Each identity must
commonly be legitimated. Legitimating one's self-structure is
like dusting an old house: if he starts by dusting the parlour,
by the time he gets to the upstairs guest room, the parlour is
already badly in need of dusting again. Women's work is never
done, nor is that of maintaining the self.

The authors here are discussing a process that may best be
observed in small group behaviour. What are we announcing to the
percipient onlooker by what we continue to do there? A proper
answer to this question calls for a protracted study of social
behaviour and for attention to the latest research conclusions. We
shall content ourselves with what has been most prominent in
students' recordings that stretch over many years.
(1) When we join any primary group we bring with us a personal
history of our membership in previous primary groups: our new
experiences will be profoundly affected by our old experiences:

> I am afraid Tom is not happy either in his work with the
> children or with the rest of the staff. It stems mostly from
> himself. He is a very insecure person who constantly needs the
> praise and support of others: is easily hurt and offended mostly
> by imaginary slights and offences: he cannot get himself out of
> the centre of the picture. It all goes back to his childhood: he
> was neglected as a child and starved of real love. He seems to be
> a standing refutation of the belief that the best social worker is
> he who has passed through the same experiences as the client.

Similarly, if Elsie was spoiled in the family, she may bring the same
expectations to the girl guide company: if John was neglected at
home, he may respond more gratefully to the care that he receives,
say, in the Sunday school. That is to say, our present experiences
may be interpreted by congruence with, or compensation for,
our previous experiences: or, perhaps more commonly, a mixture
of both with one feature more prominent. No hard and fast rules
can be made beyond one single point that the history of previous
membership in primary groups is frequently a clue to present
behaviour.
(2) When people make contact with each other—at a single
encounter or over a sustained period—they normally use a set of
social techniques where there is a large, agreed scale: and part of

this unspoken understanding is the clues they give each other.[14] To some extent, of course, everybody will have their own system of techniques and clues depending on their personality and social experiences. Argyle argues that private styles are determined partly by common factors of the other's sex, age, social class and 'warmth' or 'coldness'. Thus (p. 45):

> Some people behave so differently towards men and women that they seem to undergo a personality change when moving from one encounter to the other. A young man may be very relaxed with men, but terrified of women, or aggressive and competitive towards men and very amorous and at ease with women.

But the present argument is that there will be expectations about techniques and clues of social interaction which are part of the normative structure of the group: and a constant relevance is to consider how far any single member understands these acceptable techniques and is prepared to use them: how far he can receive and interpret the clues and is prepared to employ them himself. Usually these norms are part of the unseen, unacknowledged infrastructure, but they can be brought into view:

> After a few staff meetings, one young, newly-trained worker was involved in more and more fierce arguments about methods and philosophy. On some of these occasions he was quite rude to the Principal. Matters were brought to a head on one occasion when an older worker rebuked the newcomer with the words, 'We are not in the habit of talking to our Principal like that.'

But there are many more recordings which show that the reality is buried and must be brought to the surface for analysis.

> In looking through my recordings this morning, I was brought up against the fact that Jim is unpopular, almost an outsider— as most of the staff I think would acknowledge—yet I was not clear about the reason. There are many reasons why in fact he should be popular: he is young, personable and physically attractive. What I think is the reason became clear when I listed all the things he had said at team meetings. He really doesn't understand how we communicate with each other. He is likely to launch a frontal attack when the rest of us know we are likely to progress further by infiltrating into enemy positions. He doesn't, like longer-standing members, express his views

tentatively and give due weight to the opposition. Moreover, he doesn't pick up quickly enough the unspoken signs of disapproval—or sense the atmosphere in silence, gesture, expression. Jim's failure to understand explains a lot of his gaffes, his partial rejection and his general standing with the team.

Positively, under this heading we are looking for private strategies of social behaviour which may be employed.

I came to the conclusion that the Principal was at his most dangerous when he was most friendly! Behind this statement lies the fact that consciously or unconsciously he was at his most charming—all smiles and so on—when he was expressing disagreement with what had just been said.

(3) A favourite exercise of the students has been to judge, over a protracted period of assessment, how far the behaviour that is natural to each single member is modified by the continuing association: in other words, to measure what group pressures and expectations do to character traits in each case.

Looking back over a term's recordings on our students' group, I saw how different our behaviour was at the beginning and the end. There are many reasons for this, of course. We began as strangers and now we each have an identity for the rest. But one reason for the change is that our 'natural behaviour' has been changed by group pressures and expectations. One of us represses a natural authoritarianism because we know how this will not be acceptable. Another, although naturally shy and reticent, is ready to share her feelings with the others because she is sure of understanding and support. What I cannot be sure of is how far any one of us has been changed as people by this experience. Do we only behave in this 'new way' in the group? Have we (to quote the tutor) 'internalized these values'?

In a casework extract from Dr Button's work, we can see the process brought to a head in a manner which emphasizes the self-learning potential of groups: here group standards confront personality traits.[15]

I found the group quietly helping Sister Mary through a difficult patch. She had been disturbed by the response she had received when she had asked one of her colleagues whether

she was at all dominant: he had said mildly that she usually
got done what she intended people should do. This had been
reinforced by the fact that she had been shown as assertive in
the personality test. Although neither of these things seemed
serious in themselves, they apparently conflicted strongly with
her own self-image.

(4) There are three measurements which belong together and they
also belong to the question of the identity which the group has
for each single member:

(a) Some are centrally involved with the purpose of the group,
both for achievement and maintenance: others maintain a position
that is peripheral and an attitude that is more casual. Usually the
former see themselves as gaining more needs-satisfaction. On an
in-service training course one is always liable to have recruited a
student who is there because he is sent by his employers: he values
the course for future promotion prospects, but not for the skill
that is the end-product of the course. Being vastly experienced, he
doubts whether he has anything here to learn. Perhaps he is
suspicious of the subject and regards it as academic, fashionable
and useless. He can be discouraging to a tutor since he is reluctant
to be involved. He sits lightly to the norms and is happy to encourage any displacement of goals. Yet others are not 'group-
minded'; they are too self-opinionated to listen to the opinions of
others; they can be 'lone wolves', strong independent characters
who, to change the metaphor, 'plough a lonely furrow'.

(b) What identity has the group for the individual member? What
does he hope to gain personally from this association? As one
student commented:

> You could divide the committee into several groups according
> to the main features of its identity for them. To the county
> officials, it was a threat, a necessary aspect of democratic
> procedure, but providing 'amateurs' with an opportunity of
> appraising their work critically. To others it was 'status raising'
> since belonging to this committee was prestigious for them.
> For a few, the main satisfactions were looked for in the work
> that was to be done—making provision for a needy section of
> the community.

It is possible that in a youth centre, 90 per cent of the youngsters
are motivated to attend almost entirely by the good times they have

there: that leaves 10 per cent who also see the youth organization as making proper demands on their loyalty.

(c) How much does the member think he gains from membership? Depending on the circumstances, the answers may be under the headings of insight, healing, emotional support of various kinds and goal achievements. Ottaway quotes:[16]

> Apart from the fact that there is always someone with something interesting to say on any topic, the chief value of the group to me is to help me to be more aware of the reality of oneself, and to clarify one's thoughts in a way which would otherwise be very difficult. I, for instance, have become very aware of how much I have changed my convictions in the last few years.

(5) There are few groups which do not have their 'awkward moments'. A tactless, inappropriate remark or a personal attack on a private member, produces an atmosphere which can be unpleasant, and, indeed, threatening either to the whole or to individuals. How each individual reacts consistently to these incidents will help us to understand them much better and possibly to do something to help them on the basis of our intuitive knowledge. Some make negative reactions of hostility, aggressiveness, withdrawal or dependence: others make positive responses of fence-mending, conciliation and tension-relieving, as can be seen in the following example:

> The three speakers were invited out to lunch before the official meeting. Instead of going to a restaurant or hotel, an invitation was accepted—from one of the officials of the organizing body—to take the whole party out to lunch in the canteen of a local works. Over the meal one of the officials dropped an awful clanger. In a voice audible to the whole company, he apologized to the speakers: 'I usually look for a four-star hotel for lunch on these occasions. I am afraid this is not as good a meal as we usually provide.' There was a deafening silence. Then one man withdrew from the situation and began another conversation with his neighbour. Another said, 'That's a fine thing to say. We've done our best.' A third remarked, 'But we are all really grateful for a fine meal.'

(6) Usually over a series of gatherings, we give ourselves an identity in relation to the whole. We may in fact carry this to the

8

point where we have 'type-cast' ourselves, that is, created expectations among the others that we will continue to behave in a certain way, say, as the 'joker' of the party. This role-expectation may come to be hung around our necks, like a dead albatross, when it is secretly distasteful to us. But we may continue to behave according to the expectations because we hesitate to disappoint people and because most of us behave to a marked degree according to the expectations of others. Of course, the self-identity of the single member is usually less dramatic, consistent and immutable, but it should be grasped by the observer. An analysis of a vast quantity of students' recording among all sorts and conditions of men suggests that the majority of us do in the end see ourselves as cast for a recognizable role in the continuing drama of a group.

'Mr Recognition-Seeker' uses diverse situations to call attention to himself. A seminar about a specific problem provides the opportunity for him to recount how he succeeded in a similar dilemma: 'Mr Playboy' exhibits his lack of involvement in the group's processes. He characteristically offers the deflating remark at the precise moment when the others feel that progress is being made.

> My own standing and standards as a tutor were severely tested at the weekly session on Thursday morning. I felt the group was moving into a more hopeful period. After sailing through stormy waters we were at last in the open seas. After a period of four weeks when everybody was tight-lipped and on the defensive, we were now willing to use our own experiences to gain insight into human behaviour, to trust each other with confidences. Marion spoke for the majority when she said, 'I find this way of working is helping me to understand what makes other people tick because we are learning what makes us tick.' There were several murmurs of assent at this. But Cedric said, 'That means he [meaning the tutor] has succeeded in a subtle form of indoctrination.' To gauge the true meaning of this remark, it has to be taken strictly in context. Cedric was not being venomous: he was not expressing personal hostility against me—we have a good relationship. But taken along with other remarks that he has made in the life-history of the group, it is clear that his comment springs from the fact that he sees himself in the cast list as 'Mr Playboy'.

The title of 'Mr Fence-Mender' requires little description, being self-explanatory.

An embarrassing situation arose when Tom and Eric indulged in verbal fisticuffs both accusing the other of inflexibility. True to form, Alan tried to close the gap between the two by saying, 'I don't think either of you really mean what you have just said. Let's think about it calmly.' Alan usually sees himself as Mr Fence-Mender.

He is closely related to a rather different character—'Mr Cover-the-Cracks'. This participant works on the assumption that all sharp disagreements are, by their nature, unfortunate and to be avoided: and he sees his own function as one who preserves 'a nice atmosphere' at all costs, being ready even to pay the price of diverting the group from its proper tasks of working out basic disagreements.

At our church meeting last night, we were having a very lively debate on whether or not to operate a stewardship system of donations. (By this the members of the church agree to give a fixed percentage of their income each week, and the proceeds are used not only for the support of the church, but for donations towards helping the poorer countries of the world.) Strong arguments were put forward on both sides, although there was little personal resentment or hostility in the contributions. Then Miss Hoskins—who usually casts herself in the role of the facilitator of a monotonous friendliness between church members—made a predictable contribution: 'As Christians we ought to be ashamed of ourselves quarrelling like this.' (We were not in fact quarrelling but usefully exploring honest differences.) 'I suggest that we abandon this debate and have a prayer-meeting about it now.' A majority accepted this 'pious' suggestion with relief. So—with Miss Hoskins's help—we avoided in a fifteen minute session of public prayer, the task that was set us. We then moved on to other business having reached no decision.

'Mr Dominator', as his name implies, can never follow the lead given by others. This can take the form of manipulation by flattery, the assertion of a superior status, the right to attention, giving directions authoritatively or interrupting the contributions of others. If 'Mr Dominator' is the appointed leader, he may be found to be motivated by one of two considerations: either that he is unwilling to delegate real responsibility to others ('If you want a job doing well, you must do it yourself'): or that his basic insecurity makes it necessary for him to demonstrate that he is always in control ('There can be only one boss of this outfit').

> When I first joined the staff of the school, I was very impressed by the way in which the Headmaster presided over the staff meeting. He outlined particular problems and then asked us to give our views and suggestions. But after a few weeks, it became obvious to me that this was only a bit of democratic window-dressing. He knew beforehand what he intended to do on each of these issues and if any other proposal was put forward, he opposed it: he was often too anxious and impatient to wait before opposing it. Our Headmaster—as I subsequently learned from many events—was very status-conscious: he felt his authority was diminished if he shared any of it with his colleagues.

As the following comment from a research run by the School of Educational Studies at the University of Sussex says:[17]

> It is not surprising that 'respect' was a constant topic of discussion. Respect was seen in many different ways. Some [youth] leaders thought it was gained by the expression of their own superiority over their members. These leaders built barriers between themselves and their members in order to maintain their ascendency in all fields in the club. . . . A second group of leaders felt that they had the respect of their members when they did as they were told.

'Mr Fellow-Traveller' is a very different character: he seems to have 'left himself at home'. He makes no distinctive contribution to the encounter. He is concerned only to discern the direction of the prevailing wind and be carried along by it.

A few minor characters (who only make brief appearances on the stage of these dramas recorded by students) can be dismissed in a few lines. The susceptibilities of 'Mr Blue-Nose' are easily shocked: he is characterized equally by his frequent references to principles and his lack of warmth and humanity. 'Mr Trouble Maker', for one or more of half-a-dozen possible reasons, seems intent on destruction. 'Mr Cynical' consistently presents the view that nobody is straightforward and honest. 'Mr One-track-mind' has a product to sell, a point of view, and nothing that happens will divert him from this overriding purpose. 'Mr Egocentric' sees all events in the group in relation to himself. 'Mr Problem-Orientated' seems frightened by nothing so much as a possible solution to the problems that are encountered.

In this list there is a concentration on the more dramatic, sharply-defined roles which individual members elect to play and, on the whole, there is a concentration on negative rather than positive roles. Most groups are largely made up of 'run-of-the-mill members', utility players rather than specialists, helping the group in a measure with its task and contributing to a friendly atmosphere. But they do not stand out as our characters above stand out: hence they receive much less notice just as the respectable citizen has far less chance of seeing his name in the newspapers than the notorious criminal.

(7) The identity given to the individual by the group. A single member is not always seen by the others as he sees himself: there can be a difference between his self-image and his group-image. Indeed, painful problems of acceptance may arise for those who one day learn that they are not seen by the others as they see themselves.

> The tutorial group had been in existence for some time and, by and large, they had passed through what Ottaway calls 'the defensive stage' when they were afraid to offer their personal experiences as raw material for learning. I suggested an exercise in which each of them tried to find a word to describe the role in the group played by each including themselves. Of course, the object of the exercise is to disclose those cases where there is a conflict between self-image and group-image, and the employment of the approach requires an accurate estimate by the tutor of the levels of maturity, confidence and mutual support that have been reached. In only three cases was there any striking disparity between the two scores and for two of the participants concerned there was no painful adjustments required: they accepted the score good-humouredly and as a stimulus to self-knowledge. But Mr 'G' found it hard to swallow. As an older man he had put himself down as 'Father-figure' but the designation of his fellow-students included 'boss' and 'headmaster'. There was general laughter at the announcement of the result in which Mr 'G' tried to join but as I watched him

carefully during the rest of the session, it was evident that he was having to digest an unpleasant truth. Would he learn from this disclosure or be unduly discouraged by it?

In the film *The Loneliness of the Long-Distance Runner*, it is clear from his conversations that the Governor sees himself as a benign figure, much-loved by the boys for the benevolent interpretation of his role: but when he has moved on, it is clear from their comments that the boys see him as an instrument of authoritarian control which they resent.[18]

But the observer seeks to recognize the standing of each member with the whole, for general purposes of understanding the situation and not only that he may compare it with the self-image:

> In deciding that 'G' was the most popular member and, to some extent, the leader of the group, I was aware of his good physical appearance and pleasant disposition. . . . 'A's unhappy position was due to his very poor intelligence, his anti-authority attitudes, insolence, bad language and his complete inability to establish relationships within a group. . . . 'H' appeared to me to be the potential leader of the group until 'G' arrived. He resented 'G's popularity and his choice of 'D' is flavoured with jealousy of 'G's position.

Myself

Once again we must point to an habitual tendency for students to analyse everything within sight except themselves. Too often they see themselves as external to the enterprise, as though they are invisible observers, or unnoticed flies on the wall. They are, of course, part of the scene, affecting the group process even though they are nothing but observers: still more, of course, if they have a responsibility as workers or leader. (Here we are careful not to trespass on the territory that comes later and encloses a concentration on the subject of leadership.)

Ottaway's enterprise provided many examples of the recorder coming to terms with his own involvement.[19]

> It occurs to me that I am not sure of my role within the group. . . . In a 'learning' group there is a teacher and the rest are pupils. But this is a 'discussion group'. . . . In our group the subject matter is very personal. So I ask myself 'What have I of

value to offer? How much am I justified in taking up the time
of the group pressing this point or that?'

The same feature is reported again and again by Leslie Button.
In estimating the scene, the observer is driven in the end not to
exclude his own participation:[20]

> The previous meeting of the tutorial term had obviously made
> Ken conscious of his didactic approach to his group, and he
> seems to have replaced this by close questioning. It seems as if
> he is so keen to put over his own views that, as he has foregone
> the more direct way of doing this, he is attempting to do it, as
> it were, by proxy through the inescapable answers to his close
> questioning.

The most important feature of this part of interpreting the scene
can be described in terms of role-expectations and identity. How
do I see myself in relation to the group? (Whether as mere observer, or with some responsibility for influencing behaviour, although
we shall concentrate on the latter identity.) How, on the whole, am
I seen by the rest? What is the relation between the identity I give
myself and the identity I am given by the group? Are the role-
expectations on both sides consistent or conflicting?

The process is illustrated from the following report on practical
work in a class for maladjusted children: it displays, for an early
effort, a promising ability on the part of the student to analyse his
own experiences with a fair objectivity:

> First of all I was treated as a bit of a novelty—as all children
> treat newcomers whose job it is to help. However, I am a fairly
> aggressive and authoritative person and so would not on a
> personality level accept the noise, unrebuked, the abuse and
> uncontrolled atmosphere of the classroom. What I am now
> saying may seem very egotistical and in fact it is—but having
> thought it out carefully, I think it is near to a factual
> description. I found therefore that I was shouldering a fair
> amount of responsibility for the control of the class. This
> presented problems. However, I need not have worried about
> acquiring more authority from the teacher—for whenever I
> overstepped the mark, a child or several members of the group
> would remind me that I was not 'the teacher' and that there were
> some decisions which only he could take. . . . So then my
> personality dictated that I play a fairly strong authoritative

role but the group ensured that I moderated my
authoritativeness in some areas since I was not 'teacher'. . . .
There were several other roles I played. . . . At times I found
myself an interpreter or intermediary between child and
several children and the teacher and would say 'Of course the
teacher doesn't mean that—think about what he's saying.'

Such openness about one's identity is not always found, but lack
of it often goes along with, and is related to, a serious failure to
grasp the situation and consequent inefficiency. It is as though if
we normally exclude from scoring our own standing there is much
else that we cannot see as the following examples show:

(a) A headmaster over morning coffee was relating an encounter
with an outside agency. 'I told them I had twelve teachers working
under me.' There was a painful silence in the staffroom. The
teachers thought they were working *with* him. And thus in a casual
phrase was revealed the gap between his own identification of his
role and theirs. The headmaster had the grace to realize his error,
blushed and tried to mend a gaping hole in the fence.

(b) 'My husband doesn't want a wife, he wants a housekeeper:
my children don't want a mother but a provider', says Mrs
Charney to the marriage guidance counsellor. She is talking about
the clash of role-expectations in a primary group.

(c) A young Protestant pastor was bitterly disappointed in the
lack of response to his ministry and sought the counsel of an older
friend. In the subsequent counselling sessions, he discovered that
the main area of his problem lay in an unrealized clash of role-
expectations. He saw himself as a prophet commissioned to offer
'Divine Truth' whether his parishioners found it palatable or not,
whereas the parishioners were looking for a friend to help them
with their problems. As Protestants, he expected them to decide
spiritual issues for themselves and to subscribe to the notion of
'the priesthood of all believers': in fact, they hoped that he would
sometimes perform priestly functions for them and decide issues
which they found too difficult. After he had worked through this
issue of identity for himself in the presence of a friendly counsellor,
the young pastor somewhat changed his style of ministry and slowly
gained more acceptance.

Once again we are calling attention to the obvious. Common-
sense dictates that leaders estimate the total situation including
their own location. However that, as in other matters, the obvious

is often overlooked is demonstrated by the frequency with which trainees learn from a careful examination of this territory. For we have been arguing that failure to understand his identity is a major source of weakness: but conversely, this exercise, deliberately undertaken, is again and again a learning point for the trainee: it often seems that he must come to terms with himself before he can come to terms with the group. But not always at first directly: the insecure and inadequate can be overwhelmed by a rush of self-knowledge. There have been many instances where the only acceptable way forward was for the student to study first 'the identity problem' as it related to third parties. Then by an easier transition, he could come to himself.

There are at least two instructive examples of this approach in the Bible: walking one evening on the roof of his palace, King David saw Bathsheba, wife of Uriah, bathing. He immediately desired her for himself and subsequently arranged for Uriah to be put in the fiercest fighting of the battle where he was killed. When Nathan, the prophet, arrived to confront David with his sin, he did not begin with a frontal attack. He told a story of a rich man who had robbed a poor man of his meagre possessions. David was very angry and cried out, 'As the Lord lives, the man who did this deserves to die.' 'You are the man,' said Nathan. And David admitted his fault.[21]

Painful self-identification is facilitated—here and in the training course—by first recognizing our faults in others. Jesus several times uses the same method. For example, he wished to bring home to the overtly religious people of his day, the mean part they were playing in being resentful and not rejoicing when the notoriously disreputable people were attracted by his teaching. But a direct description would have been too painful for them and have created resistance. So he told a story, which held their attention for its sheer interest, but also contained the sting at the end—'Thou art the man.' 'Another time, the tax-gatherers and other bad characters were all crowding in to listen to him: and the Pharisees and the doctors of law began grumbling among themselves. "This fellow", they said, "welcomes sinners and eats with them." He answered them with this parable . . .':[22] and the parable was that of The Prodigal Son, although it ought to be 'The Elder Brother' since he surely is the main character. There would be at least a few of the critics who listened to the story, found themselves condemning the meanness of the older boy, only to see, too late, that they had admitted a fresh insight into their own identity in the life-situation.

Of course, it is in much less dramatic and less salutary ways that the tutor uses this approach with trainees, but the principle is the same. There can be a quick and easy transition from analysing other role-incumbents to analysing oneself, even though unacceptable elements may be involved.[23]

Grasping the relationship between our own self-image and that of the group, is only one part of the task of interpretation. We have to learn the meaning of the clues in group behaviour: they will not always lie on the surface, as can be seen from the following examples:

Example 1   'At first I was worried by the increase in bad behaviour when I was left in charge of the group. They were rude to me and quite uncontrolled. At first I thought they were just taking advantage of my being new and young. But after a few days I became quite depressed and wondered whether I was training for the right job. But I began to feel better and more hopeful after a short talk with an older worker. She pointed out that the youngsters needed to test me out in this way. Some of the bad behaviour was to find out what sort of a person I was. They needed to do this since at first they didn't know where they were with me. Just, she said, as a dog coming into a strange room, sniffs around to orientate himself to the setting.'

Example 2   'I do not usually discuss the private affairs of club members with their parents. The danger is that one appears to be treating them as though they were still children. But Maisie asked me to visit her home and talk to her father (a widower) to gain his permission for her to join in the club holiday. Afterwards during the course of the evening, she pressed two questions on me at various times, which I thought were revealing: "You are not taking his side, are you?" and "Did you like my Dad?" It seems that she wants me to be an adult who confirms her feeling for her father but who will develop an adult relationship with her.'

Example 3   ' "Would you still try to help me if I stole from here?" Johnny's question worried me. He was on probation for stealing but we had been happy for him to join the club. Was he trying me out? Was he reacting with natural dislike to somebody who was there "to help him"? When I knew him better, I realized he was saying, "Will you be for me the kind of adult who would still want to help me even if 'I did wrong' again?"'

Example 4 'We tape-recorded a whole training session and played it back to ourselves afterwards. There was much self-conscious laughter, though during the actual seminar we had largely forgotten about the "mike" and had become absorbed in the subject. But Hector, usually very vocal, was unusually quiet during the play-back. Afterwards, as we walked down the steps to coffee he said to me [tutor] privately, "I never realized before that I spoke so often, so loudly or with such domination. I thought I was the facilitator. I realize for the first time how the others must see me."'

Throughout this present chapter, we have used the space available on interpretation to look at the matter in terms of roles rather than processes; to use, so to speak, the nouns of the subject rather than the verbs. In my tutorial experience this is a more practical approach for most students. But it would in fact have been possible to have written the whole of this chapter putting the emphasis on the processes and allowing the roles to emerge as a by-product. For those to whom this method might have appealed more, there are several accounts that are readily available.[24]

A simple and useful schedule could be:

1 How did this group come together?
2 Why did it come together?
3 What brings the group together?
4 Have the reasons changed at all?
5 What decisions did the group make?
6 What action has the group planned, if any?
7 Who are the leaders of the group? Why? Where does their authority lie?
8 What was the experience of each member in the group?
9 How did the members communicate with each other?
10 Were there any sub-groups, temporary or permanent?

5 Action

This book is chiefly about action. All that has gone before is
intended to contribute to the moment when the group worker has
to do something. We hope that the suggested exercises have
encouraged sensitivity and fostered an informed intuition. But it is,
of course, true that the only valid criterion for training courses of
this kind is whether they produce more efficient group workers.
Admittedly, such courses are by no means successful. A common
gap lies between the student's grasp of theoretical concepts and his
application of these theories to the group with which he is working.
For professionals in training, the only hope of progress lies in a
lavish provision of skilled supervision; as the present work is for
non-professionals, we must rely on the descriptions of as many
real-life situations as possible.

One student in his recording judged that the action taken by
residential staff (in the sense of the arrangements they make for
children) is mistaken.

> As soon as they were inside the door, they were told it was
> teatime. I feel a little more time to settle down would have
> helped for although the children wanted their food, an
> impression was given that the workers wanted to get tea over
> as soon as possible since it was usually a very unruly session.

Another student follows his assessment of a situation with a
deliberate plan of action.

> As a result of my observations and interpretations I then posed
> myself the question 'what can I do now to encourage good
> personal relationships within the group?' I confined my efforts
> to diverting some of the hostility away from 'B' and 'C' and
> helping them to play a more positive role in the group. I
> quickly noticed that 'B' had some ability in the sporting field;
> so I concentrated on involving 'B' in group games where he was
> able to command an important role and gain the respect of the
> other members. In 'C's case I decided that his most essential
> requirement was self-confidence. . . . I consciously gave him
> much attention in a personal way.

Both students were correct in their attempts to make a judgment about the appropriate action in these cases; but it is equally important for us to see that the rest of us cannot know with any certainty whether their judgments were right; simply because we do not know, neither were we involved with, the circumstances. Students are sometimes a little disappointed when they discover that on a training course they cannot be given a rule book for group work, a sort of ready reckoner for handy reference. The opening paragraph of this chapter may well have raised hopes in some readers' minds which we now are about to say cannot be fulfilled. Alas, we cannot offer a blueprint, only guidelines, and a little reflection will convince us that this is inevitable. The circumstances, goals and resources of groups vary so widely that it is only possible to enunciate a few principles and ask that their possibilities be exploited on the occasion. (To repeat a previous point—this reality is fully demonstrated when students begin to use their own recordings and casework for training. They are now familiar with a wide range of circumstances and all view the scene in two dimensions. Other people's material, however professional, lacks the detailed personal knowledge to make it useful.) We may say that the general aim of our action is to facilitate a process by which each member of the group gains in some definable way by the presence of the others.

We may also say that our group worker will make sure that he has a clear intelligence of the main purpose of the enterprise. Once again, as in much training material on this subject, this sounds banal. It would hardly be worth saying, were it not for the fact that many tutors on in-service courses for social workers and educationalists find a lack of clear purpose among their students a conspicuous factor. To quote the Youth Service Research Project of the University of Sussex: 'They [the part-time youth leaders] began with no clear definitions of what their role was to be, and many had never had the opportunity to discover either the original aims of their youth group, or to establish any clear rationale for the existence of the group.'[1] Leslie Button comments of his group workers that:[2]

When they searched into their own organisations many were completely unable to state any real goals entertained by their main groups (as distinct from the ambitions of their leaders). Others, who had thought that there were clear goals in their organisation, discovered on looking deeper that it was quite possible that their members did not subscribe to these goals, and in any case had not been asked.

We may say that our group worker should give some thought to the best methods of achieving these goals though it be in the long-term again. It is sad to learn that even those who have clear objectives may be found to be relying upon 'hit and miss' methods to achieve them.

In contrast with the officers at the centre where I work, I could not help noticing that the managers of the licensed discotheque had clear objectives. They wanted a happy place that could be profitable. They had also given attention to means. I asked one of them 'What do you do when your place becomes unfashionable and attendances drop off?' He replied immediately, 'Two things. We distribute a lot of free tickets in the city. We close a number of grilles and those who are present become compressed into a smaller area and everybody gets the impression that we are fairly crowded-out.' I could not help reflecting that still 'the children of darkness' are often wiser than the children of light!

We may say that almost always the group worker is concerned with the twin tasks of maintenance and achievement, the expressive and the task aspects of the affiliation in varying proportions. For as Homans has pointed out,[3] those who share tasks together will grow sentiments about each other; but equally, those who like each other will be more disposed to share tasks.

A friend of mine is convinced that what made his a really united family was the fact that they literally built their own house. On the other hand, I know families so divided that they would never lay the first brick. Co-operative effort is usually both an expression of, and itself creates, group feeling and the group worker needs to know in what proportions the ingredients are mixed. Michael Argyle notes:[4]

The primary goal of the supervisors [in industry] is to get the work done, but an important secondary goal is to keep the team satisfied—otherwise there will be absenteeism, labour turnover and a general lack of co-operation. Supervisors may fail in a number of ways of which the most common are:

relying too much on formal power; not giving enough
direction; so that other members of the group assume
leadership; producing high output but low job satisfaction.

In identifying these principles of action so far, are we going
beyond common-sense? Have we indicated any line of action which
would not be taken by any wise, experienced and sensitive
person? For the role of the professional, the answer may be clear:
a specialized training and often a supervisory service raises the
levels of performance. But we claim that training, on a necessarily
part-time basis, is profitable also for the non-professional. To his
inherited assets—the traditions of the organization in which he
works, the resources of the members involved and his personal
gifts—he can add an awareness of group processes and a knowledge
of techniques which have proved useful in similar circumstances.
This is what we hope to demonstrate in the illustrations from
various practical situations which follow later in these chapters;
they are documentary, not fictional; they are based on the author's
extended service as a group worker and a tutor, rather than on
theoretical writings on the subject.

Another cautionary word is inserted here. In answer to the
question which trainees are prone to ask, 'What am I to do?' the
answer very often is 'Nothing'. Again and again, the wisest
course is to leave the group process to develop; observe them but
do not intervene.

A recurring 'problem' of training is the attitude of the student
who feels compelled to do something about every situation in
which he is involved. ('Playing God' is how it is described sometimes by other students in the training group.) He is likely to have
been reared in a religious atmosphere, and in many ways this can
have been an advantage, but in this case, it has led to a 'missionary,
moralistic, paternalistic and over-protective' attitude, especially
to those in need, over whom he has authority. Or it may simply
be that the student has a psychological need to be an activist and
lacks the security to allow the participants to develop their own
resources.

Serious with all social groups, this fault can be disastrous when
the clients are 'young adults' since they are at a developmental
stage when the right of self-determination and the chance to work
things out for themselves is vital for their emotional maturation.
But many adults are reluctant to give them enough space to make

their own mistakes. Characteristic of adult attitudes is a parent
reported upon by Doris Odlum:[5]

> One mother assured me that she never interfered with her son
> and could not imagine why he had become so withdrawn and
> secretive. She told me 'When he wanted to bring his
> girlfriend home I said to him; "Now I never interfere and you
> must make your own choice, but I can see that she is not at
> all the girl for you and if you marry her you will never have
> a moment's happiness." '

Young adults, however, are not the only people who are flashing
to the group worker a message similar to that left behind for his
sponsors by an Arctic explorer; 'Please do not rescue me prematurely.' In fact, skilful action is based on a nice calculation
between intervention and non-intervention; the effective group
worker knows when to be active and when to be passive; he knows
that the 'client' needs both permission and support, and he is
able to mix the ingredients in the right proportions.

Instructive in this regard is an ancient simile which comes from
the Bible (Deuteronomy 32:11-12). The mother-eagle stirs her
nest and the young ones fall out, apparently to their destruction.
There is method in this madness: the infant eagles, under dire
necessity, learn to use their wings, but they have not much strength
and soon they are exhausted. But their mother, with matchless eye,
has been watching for this moment and swoops below them and
carries them on her pinions. The mother-eagle can be instructive
for us because although she never does for them what they can
do for themselves, she is swift and eager to do for them what they
cannot do for themselves.

A much more recent and 'scientific' account of the same conduct
is contained in the writings of T. R. Batten.[6] In the directive
approach, the group worker proceeds on the assumption that he
knows what is good for the 'client'; if there is resistance, he looks
around for more subtle ways of 'selling his goods'; but he does not
question whether he is trying to sell the right goods. In the non-
directive approach, the 'client' is helped to define his own needs
and to organize resources to satisfy them. Dr Batten is careful to
point out that neither approach is infallibly and invariably right
for every situation, although most of us, for a number of reasons,
have a gravitational pull towards the second. But his plea is for
community workers who have the skill to use the approach

which fits the occasion, which is an application of our argument that the efficient operator knows when to be active and when to be passive.

One canon, however, may be said to apply to all occasions for the exercise of this skill: action should always include a recording process. Is this a reasonable dogma when we have previously affirmed that our attention is focused on the widest possible interpretation of the term 'group worker', including parents? Is it feasible, is it even natural, that the mother should be keeping a careful record of the interactions within her family, making a note of what Tommy said and how Mary looked? Perhaps mothers are so close to the events of the family and so constantly with its members, that they can carry it all in their heads. But two things may be said. One is that there was a time when English women of a certain social class did in fact habitually undertake a recording of family events; they entered it in a diary and it did provide the raw material for recall of and reflection upon family interactions and development. And many such accounts sought to be as objective as possible so that for the future recollection of events, one was not relying upon a memory susceptible to the practice of distortion; indeed, the singular merit of a private diary was that it could be written under conditions that encouraged openness and frankness. The second point about a mother is that she may be among the few 'group workers' whose closeness to the events makes her mental reconstruction of them sufficient for purposes of recall and reflection, the two functions which form the basis of the recording process.

There is not one sovereign method for everybody; each group worker must in the end find the style most useful to himself. Some work best on a narrative approach; others prefer a schedule with divisions like Facts, Group Behaviour, Sub-groups, Individuals, Myself, and Future Action. Here we use our space to describe one or two of the principles of recording and use the references to indicate where examples, systems and schedules can be found.[7]

(a) One purpose of a recording is to be an *aide-mémoire*, to remind the group worker to do what he may easily forget. Where this aim is prominent, the account has to be comprehensive.

(b) But a more valuable purpose of recording is as a device for self-training; in the recall, we can reflect upon the events and seek to understand what is happening here; we can take thought before

9

future action; we can assess our own performance and hope to improve it. A shorter recording may serve this purpose; a ten-minute scrutiny may provide enough information for self-examination.

These first two points are concerned with the 'why' of recording. It is a tool for the job—helping us to penetrate beneath the surface and see what is happening there—helping us to stop and consider in some situations what is the best course when spontaneous reactions are inadequate. It is a tool for self-training—helping us to assess our own behaviour and feelings, the influence we are having, the opportunities we are missing and so to raise our performance by healthy self-criticism.

(c) This brings us to the 'what' of recording; obviously not everything. The content is decided by the purpose. It is a different exercise from the keeping of records that may be required by our employers; one difference is that this account is confidential, for our eyes alone; it is the prelude to understanding action and growing skill and the material is selected on this basis.

(d) Under the heading of 'how', we have already said that each group worker, whilst satisfying the standards outlined above, should find the best technique for himself, after a period, maybe, of trial and error. But here also there are principles of fairly general application. The account should be as close to the events as possible. Normally, those who are observed are unaware of the scrutiny. Before too long, the recording should be reflected upon for the meanings it has to yield to us.

The following group situations are divided according to their primary objectives. (A very common one—the committee—has been omitted since it has been extensively used in an earlier section for illustrative purposes.) General principles informing action, previously enunciated, apply to all of them, but in the paragraphs that follow the writer, on the basis of an extensive experience as a group worker and tutor, indicates what particular lines of action seem most frequently to be called for in these different situations.

A The discussion group

It can be formal—the set-piece—or informal—the spontaneous airing of a question which arises in the bar or the canteen. Ideally, the educational aim is that all shall profit by listening to the views of others and receiving their information on the subject. We are assuming that the group worker has some responsibility of leadership which may be true even in the informal situation. A father will probably have more authority and responsibility in a family discussion. A youth leader will be distinguished from the club member and perhaps be expected to give a lead. The following are suggestions for improved performance as a group leader:

(a) Help to create a warm, friendly atmosphere using as appropriate words, gestures and expressions, and throughout, show respect for all and be open to criticism.

(b) If you have to initiate the discussion in a formal session, think of ways to create interest. Do you choose the subject? Then 'Is there a hell?' is better than 'Our ultimate accountability'. Are there any visual aids to put up or hand around? If you start the discussion, then aim to open the subject not to close it. Leave loose ends. A good technique is to end your introduction with a question which demands more than a 'Yes' or 'No' answer. Thus, to use Haiman's examples[8]—'Mrs Phillips, if you were confronted with a choice between salvation and degradation, which would you choose?'— is obviously bad. The poor lady can only give one answer. Similarly—'Jane, do you believe that college authorities have a right to exclude certain girls from membership because of their race or religion?'—is bad. Jane can only answer 'Yes' or 'No'; whereas—'As you understand it, Mr Martin, what is involved in the proposal for consolidating our departments and how do you feel about it?'—is good. He is invited to take part and made to feel that his views will be welcome.

(c) A whole series of actions are unified by the biggest commandment for the discussion group leader—let the group do the work. One is to tolerate silences and not find them embarrassing (failure to do this is the most frequent defect of the novice and the untrained) since in the silence the group is compelled to develop its own resources. Visiting speakers who invite contributions from the audience when they have finished often suffer at the hands of uncomprehending chairmen in this regard. These chairmen judge that a silence after the invitation to join in is uncomplimentary to the speaker and may foolishly try to protect him with inanities like 'Now who is going to be the first to break the ice?' or 'Whilst you are gathering your thoughts, I will ask a question.' A longer wait will usually produce a relevant discussion; if none comes, then it looks as though the conditions are not right for it, or there is nothing they want to discuss; strong pressures to participate as a presumed face-saving device for the speaker will serve no useful purpose.

There are many other examples where the necessary 'passivity' of the discussion group leader is overlooked. Some intervene too emphatically and too often because they are sure they themselves know the answer and they are fearful that the members will fall into disastrous error; or they may wish to avoid any semblance of conflict which they see as a dire threat to the stability and happiness of the enterprise.

(d) But this does not mean that the role is passive; the discussion group leader is commonly required to intervene in one or more of the following areas as required:

(i) Persuading the group not to wander too far or for too long from the subject; and not subtly changing the nature of the task. At various points he may have to help them not to evade the challenge of what they have set themselves.

(ii) Interpreting individual contributions which are visibly not understood by all.

(iii) Helping the shy and inhibited to put what they have into the general pool; gently dissuading the exhibitionist and extrovert from dominance.

(iv) Summarizing at various stages where they may be in danger of missing the wood for the trees.

(v) Protecting any who are subject to hurtful and unfair attack.

(vi) Clockwatching and ensuring a proper conclusion.

B Staff meeting

Here, in my view, is the most notorious loss of opportunity in small gatherings. Again and again students, in reporting about their practical work placements, emphasize their disappointment with the staff meeting in the establishments to which they have been sent. They find it too formal, superficial and too dominated by a hierarchical structure. When every allowance is made for the tendency of young students to look for something outside themselves to blame, it seems that the staff meeting is not often seen positively as a team gathering and an opportunity for mutual training. And knowledge of staff meetings in other and diverse organizations supports this view.

In almost every type of organization, the staff meeting, ideally, can be a principal means of goal achievement, job-satisfaction and ongoing, in-service training. A number of people can meet together to share their problems, to share insight, skills and perplexities, to talk over their real concerns and to give each other the required support. That the staff meeting rarely lives up to these high hopes is due not only to the difficulties inherent in the confrontation—likes and dislikes, fears and prejudices—but also to a widespread failure to see the possibilities by those who are mainly responsible for the exercise.

As most of the fault then seems commonly to lie with the 'man in charge'—whether headmaster, principal or 'boss'—our suggestions for improved performance will be addressed to him:

(a) Discourage everything in yourself and others which inhibits anybody from a courteous expression of their thoughts, feelings, fears, hopes and suggestions. Let's begin with you. Of course, you need the proper authority of your office—but are you inclined to rely on the prestige of your office rather than the esteem you have won by the means of your discharge of that office? Do you use your position as a protective shield? Are you a threat to the others? Do you judge contributions on their merits irrespective of their source? Real listening to each and status-raising remarks should spring—not from a self-conscious technique which will soon be detected and despised—but from a genuine respect: 'You know more about this than the rest of us. What do you think, Joe?'

(b) Where the 'boss' ceases to be gratuitously status-conscious, then it is possible that all the hierarchical rigidities will be loosened; others lower down the ladder will not be so conscious of their position. The result may be a greater amount of openness and far more communications up and down the authority ladder. We then have an organic system of communication where ideas are fed in from every level, rather than a mechanistic system where ideas only move downwards from above:

'Under the chairmanship of the chief, we were able to express feelings and misgivings that we had not been able to bring into the open under the old, more authoritarian, regime.
Of course, it took us some time to come to this position. I am sure we were helped because on several occasions our new leader shared with us his own misgivings and inadequacies.

We felt much more confident to let our own problems see the light of day and to contribute our own ideas to the various questions that were brought up at the staff meeting.'

A contrasted experience reveals a youth worker unable to bring his real feelings into the open and receive help with his dilemma:

'The general impression I get is that others see me as a good leader with few problems. I find it very hard to let them know the truth about me. They all seem so competent in their clubs. I feel I am the only one who ever does anything badly. Perhaps they all feel the same but no one ever admits it.'

(c) But the most common deficiency is the failure to use the staff meeting as a theatre for a two-way communication of both information and values:

'We were always discovering that our principal was withholding from the staff a piece of information which had been sent to him as head of the organization; not wilfully, or of malice aforethought, but simply forgetting. I suppose in the deepest sense a failure to communicate vital information is a failure to love. Our principal did not hate, but he lacked the emotional resources to love. And his lack of affection led to a lack of efficiency. We could not work well together as a team.'

'At his farewell sermon, our parson used the opportunity to scold us in his sermon. We had been, he said, an introverted community, caring only for ourselves. But the mission of the church was to the world outside. I could not help reflecting that although during his ministry with us he had met many small groups, there were few occasions on which he had discussed this purpose of the church with us.'

(d) One debilitating effect of this lack of communication is the role-ambiguity from which many people suffer in a vast range of organizations. When we enquire about this, we find the facts at first unbelievable. It seems there are multitudes carrying responsibility who have not been told what is expected of them and cannot define their role. We have already quoted from the Youth Service Research Project of the School of Educational Studies at the University of Sussex. One of their sad and recurring discoveries is the role-ambiguity of the men and women who devote part of their leisure to working in youth clubs. It is clear that there are either no team meetings, or if there are, they do not help in role-definition (see pp. 5 and 6).

(e) Those who preside over staff meetings may have to give careful thought to the nature of their relationships with colleagues; the aim is the right mixture of personal and professional elements. Too much of the first and not only is the team in danger of becoming too interaction-orientated, with too great an interest in itself and not in the work to be done; but also, the leader may allow his necessary authority to erode. A few recordings suggest staff meetings where the leader cannot play his role because in general there is not enough social distance between him and the rest.

> After a few weeks, I became convinced that the principal's difficulty in the staff meeting was that he was so much one of the boys on other occasions. I am not referring to his friendliness with the staff but his constant frivolity, not to mention buffoonery. I am sure he did it with the best intentions but the result was that in the staff meeting, we could not or would not let him wear another hat.

Where, in the opposite extreme, the professional element is too strongly mixed in the relationship, the affective links will be missing; and this can diminish loyalty and trust, hence reducing the effectiveness and productivity of the group. The following recording, although slightly 'catty', hints at this situation.

> The Head would have been far more effective if only in his social relationships with his colleagues he could sometimes have forgotten that he was the Head. Even had he been able to do this, I doubt whether his wife would have encouraged him. Tom spoke for all of us one day when he said, 'He'd get on much better if only he would have a night out with the boys.'

C Groups for fostering personal relationships

For some groups the primary goal is the development of personal relationships. There may be a product, but it is not the criterion of success. At the end, we may cheerfully admit that a stated objective was not reached, but the enterprise was justified by the fun, and the enrichment of our lives, above all because 'we have got to know so-and-so a lot better'. In these circumstances we feel that it is truly better to travel hopefully than to arrive.

Of course, one of the most widespread examples in modern societies is the nuclear family, especially at the stage where the children are young; later when they are young adults, the family may become more task-orientated on their behalf as they need support to make their own way in the world. But although parents will speak with immense pride of the achievements of their offspring, they are equally likely to say with satisfaction, 'Ours has always been a happy family.'

This does not mean that there is not a task-orientation in most family groups. In fact, a widely accepted view is that the father is traditionally the task-leader in the home, preparing the youngster for his struggle with the world and concerned to encourage skill, courage and knowledge; whereas the mother is seen as the expressive leader concerned with personal relationships, love and tenderness. But in the early stages at least, the creation of a fellowship is likely to have priority. Also true is the fact that parents are normally concerned about the individual development of each child, but obviously not in isolation from the others.

Families are the most common but not the only example of this type of association; the old-fashioned class or fellowship meeting in non-conformist churches also had this primary objective in a religious context. It also figures prominently in the role of the 'detached youth worker', that is, one who works with socially-needy youngsters in a non-judgmental way, on the streets, rather than by inviting them to a centre with a commitment to a set of norms. It we quote an example of this type of enterprise we can see that in a sense it is a 'blow-up' of the pictures of a mother with a family of small children, since they both seek the building of personal relationships with those who are in the process of being socialized.

The following illustration, abbreviated from Goetschius and Tash, illustrates the relations between the roles:[9] Susan, the group worker, is meeting with ten girls, all of whom are members of large families living in overcrowded homes; most of them are on probation for non-attendance at school or petty theft. There were many tensions in the group; heavy demands made upon the group worker by individuals; repeated fighting and actions of aggression. Susan is mainly concerned, as is a mother with a small family, to help individuals in their relationships with each other as a feature of personal development. The following are extracts from Susan's work records:

Extract 1 'Marie began to peel potatoes in the kitchen with Angela's help. Jacqueline, Sheila, Gillian and Jose were making coffee. Everyone was in the kitchen where it was warmest and there was a pleasant, noisy atmosphere of bustle and activity. Angela began to demand that the cooks be left in the kitchen alone and that everyone else go into the other room and the door be closed. I didn't want to break up the group at that moment and so persuaded Angela to leave the door open, saying that the kitchen was warmest and that everyone wanted to be near the fire. She accepted this grudgingly and gradually she gave up whining. Myra and Jane arrived with the record player and instructions that only those two, plus Sheila and Jose, were allowed to use it in case it got broken. I changed the plug, and they were impatient whilst I did it, and then dancing began in the main room. Jose with Myra, Sheila, Gillian and Jacqueline flitted from one room to the other, and from group to group and often talked to me in the kitchen. Sheila rushed into the kitchen, her face glowing, shouting "I feel mad, Miss. I feel mad", flinging her arms in the air, and pirouetting around. I replied "Well, you can be mad if you like" and she dashed back into the other room, leaping about to the music with Jose, Sheila and Jacqueline. Larks began and a lot of giggling.

'The chips began to appear from the kitchen and I received mine first and I thanked Angela saying they were very good—which they were. I could see that although they were able to organize themselves over the cooking, the distribution would be too difficult for them, so I helped them find plates and cutlery and see who wanted what, as if taking orders in a café. There were no serious quarrels, although Angela had tried too hard to organize everybody and get everybody sorted out, and she was fed up when it didn't work. Jose, Gillian, Sheila and Myra got up on the window seat and began to mime "Bobby's Girl" and Marie stood in the doorway longing to join in, butting in and telling them how to do it, so I suggested that perhaps she could be the compère and introduce the "Four Seasons" as they wanted to be called. Then Jane, and Rita also wanted to do something, but they were afraid to make the effort, so when the others' song had ended. I casually mentioned that "Bachelor Boy" was a good song to mime to and they straight away said "yes". It was their turn and

Marie joined them. Angela was looking from the kitchen and asked to join in but they said "no", as it was just for the three of them, so I said maybe she could introduce them and she did, but found it hard to withdraw when her bit was over. Jacqueline and I were the audience. Marie suddenly realized that she had not had any chips and a row was imminent because she had done the cooking all evening and she was "starved". Angela's were in the pan and I could see that Marie would be taking them, so I told her I would cook her chips and I dried them and put them on. She was pleased and quietened down and the quarrel with Angela was avoided.'

Extract 2 'Marie and Rita had to go home early and just as they were leaving Jane whispered that Marie had the bottle of shampoo. Now that I knew about it, I had to do something so I called Marie back and when we were alone, asked her about it. She produced the bottle from under her coat saying she only had a little. I said that if she wanted it she only had to ask and it would be all right. Apparently, Sheila also had some, and then Jane asked. Myra wanted the bottle of vinegar and Angela asked for the rest of the cooking fat. With the exodus of the two girls there were only six left and Jacqueline and Sheila began to do ballet dancing. Jane and Jose joined in.'

Extract 3 'Angela swept up the room and as we had the record player to take back and it was thick fog, we decided to have a taxi. Angela asked me to call for her as I do Jean and I said that Jean was on my route and she wasn't, so that I was very sorry I couldn't.'

Like a good mother, Susan:
(a) participates in and guides activities to help individuals in their relationships in the group;
(b) offers to those who feel 'left out'—for example, Marie and Gillian—a personal attention, giving relationships with herself, which may help establish other relationships in the group. Notice that she quickly withdraws, leaving the girls in the group again;
(c) accepts them still when they do things she would not do, as in the case of the shampoo. (Mothers act clean contrary to this if they say 'Mummy won't love you if . . .');
(d) refuses to be a 'doormat' for them, doesn't lose her own

integrity, doesn't over-identify with them, 'so that I was sorry I couldn't' (Some mothers serve their children ill by sacrificing too much for them; almost sinking their individuality in being mothers);

(e) protects the group from the threatened dominance of one member (Angela);

(f) satisfies the needs of individual members, encouraging them to respond in a new security to give and take of relationships.

D Groups for training

Clearly here we mean training for skill in an aspect of personal relationships—teachers, social and community workers—since training in technical skills has a larger subject content.

For these roles, it is widely acknowledged today that there are three constituent elements in an effective training course.

(a) Knowledge. This could well include a study of human behaviour at an individual and social level; a history of the provision with which we are concerned and a history of the thinking about it.

(b) Personal development—since all community roles make demands upon the emotional maturity of the worker.

(c) Development of practical skill in the role.

Although these three are put under separate headings, they are inextricably bound together. To take but one of the possible permutations—a mature person has a better chance of developing his practical skill.

Now group methods apply to all three categories. One way to study, say, a text book on sociology—and a method proven in experience—is with a small band of students each of whom introduces a chapter at succeeding sessions preparatory to a general discussion. But the group studies occupy central ground in relation to the development of personality and practical skills— central ground which unites both territories.

As the tutor meets his class for the first time, he should be saying to himself, 'You have more to learn from each other than from me.' It seems curious that for many decades it was believed that community workers could be trained for a skill by being lectured at; instead of through exposure to their own needs, development of their own resources and learning by doing; all of these gaining life and breath in the group. An ancient Chinese proverb put the matter succinctly: 'What I hear, I forget; what I see, I remember; what I do, I know.'

For an exercise of this nature, the group worker is concerned to facilitate several processes that may contribute to the twin objectives of personality development and increase in skill:

(a) The use of their efforts in practical placements as material for reflection and objective assessment. An ounce of their first-hand case work material is, for training purposes, worth a ton of second-hand material from books, however erudite. We can learn best from what we ourselves have experienced.

(b) The student's discovery, through this means, of his own inadequacy in the performance of this role, and hence of his own needs. For there is, strictly speaking, no such thing as a 'trainer of community workers'. All training is self-training and the trainer is there only to facilitate and help along a process that is largely initiated by the trainee, and to make available resources that the trainee knows that he needs. Criticism from others can be resented and prove counter-productive; self-criticism, within wide limits, leads to the desire to improve.

(c) The creation of an atmosphere of trust, confidence and support that will encourage the trainee to exposure to group examination. In this respect one usually finds the group passing through several stages. At first they may be tight-lipped, feel threatened, reluctant to reveal their true feelings and determined to talk about 'safe subjects', that is, those which do not touch them personally. The 'log-jam' may last for several weeks. The change, if it comes, may be sudden and dramatic, or so slow and gradual as to be almost imperceptible. But whatever the pace of the development the tutor may have an active part to play in it; encouraging contributions which create trust; giving support to any who suddenly feel over-exposed; even on occasions sharing with the students his own feelings of inadequacy. But the learning process is inhibited until there is a general willingness to share our negative emotions of aggressiveness, jealousy, status-seeking and inferiority.

(d) The generation of confidence for each trainee to trust in his own conclusions and to develop his own resources. Group tutors should help the student to this end because throughout they have a fundamental respect for the student, for his individuality and integrity; valuing his experiences and helping the student to build on them whilst his judgments are chastened in the group. 'No man can reveal to you ought but that which already lies asleep in the dawning of your knowledge. If he is indeed wise he does not bid you enter the house of his wisdom but rather leads you to the threshold of your own mind' (Kahlil Gibron, tenth-century philosopher).[10]

E Groups for healing

This section is not, let it be said at once, about associations for the cure of physical illnesses. No doubt there are such associations but the writer has no first-hand knowledge of them. However, there are also groups where the primary objective is to heal the participants of an emotional disturbance, inadequacy or maladjustment; and these are our present concern.

Some of these enterprises are highly technical operations undertaken by professionals, as when the psychiatrist meets a number of patients in a mental hospital and an attempt is made to forward a process of group psychotherapy by everybody being encouraged to talk through his problem in the presence of the rest, who may be able to help the patient to gain insight into his dilemma under the skilled guidance of the doctor.

Group methods have also been used in prisons in an attempt to help the inmates to understand their problems and adjust to society, as well as providing social life and the possibility of new points of contact between prisoners and warders.[11]

In parts of the USA they are experimenting with 'encounter' groups when the basic notion is that many depressed people can only be relieved from their social isolation and inadequacy by having close physical contact—hugging, for example—with their fellows. Their reply to the obvious criticism is that the group nature of the exercise keeps the activity from acquiring a sexual content.

Apart from these specialized examples, non-professionals may easily find themselves in a situation where they are responsible for encouraging a group process to help individuals in their social and emotional adjustment. They visit a disorganized family where hopelessness and apathy are the end products of years of discouragement. Or they may find that their own family has moved into a period of problem orientation. As teachers or social workers they are confronted by youngsters who are having more than average difficulty in growing up.

Although the situations described above may differ profoundly, they often have common features important both for diagnosis and for treatment:

(1) A generic title for people who are psychologically inadequate for the demands made upon them is 'the can't copes'. For example, after a short experience as a prison visitor, this is the conclusion I reached about the majority of the inmates. They were not especially wicked but they lacked the emotional resources commensurate with their duties.

'Can't copes' is in fact the title given by Goetschius and Tash to the members of their constituency,[12] adolescents who were attracted to a Paddington coffee bar by the opportunity of talking to a sympathetic social worker. Although these authors divide their constituents into different categories according to the seriousness of their plight, generally speaking they are characterized by inadequacies in family life, work situations and the building of stable personal relationships.

The inescapable corollary of this statement is that any successful group work will help them to cope better.

(2) With saddening frequency we learn that the 'can't copes' are those for whom social hunger and social ignorance go together. If they were not so socially hungry—above the rest of us—then it would not be so serious that they were socially inept; if they were socially more skilful they would know how and where to satisfy their social needs. But in them, social hunger and social ignorance continuously reinforce each other. Most of us have been fortunate enough to have been brought up in homes where we have acquired some skill in being acceptable to others around us; the 'can't copes' are almost always found to have been deprived in this place.[13]

(3) To put the matter baldly, the group worker here is seeking to create for the maladjusted member a wide tolerance of any social behaviour which is inevitable for him; ideally a tolerance which offers acceptance on any terms. As Josephine Klein says:[14]

> The group tolerates him whilst he tries out alternative ways until he finds out what is congenial to him and acceptable to others. The behaviour acceptable to others may, when first tried out by the individual, be 'external' to him. Newly-learned ways are consciously and effortfully adhered to and only later become unquestioned and habitual; 'internalised'. Paradoxically, having become part of the personality, they

make the person less dependent on the group than he was before.

Thus, in the therapeutic group, social skill may grow and the pangs of social hunger be assuaged. There are times in fact when it seems as though the member has gone back in time and is enjoying and profiting by the experience he should have had in family life. Again, according to Josephine Klein:[15]

> It is in the family that he learns that he is a valued person; here what he does and what he says is encouraged and approved. It is this which gives him the conviction he is valued. He also learns that others are pleased when he interacts with them; his expression of himself enhances their individuality and worth. It is this which gives him the conviction that self-expression on his part is gratifying to others. Within the family, assurances of worth are exchanged between socially and emotionally interdependent persons when each is expressing himself.
>   As the child is socialised, he comes to share the outlook of his family. He learns to laugh at what they think funny, to approve what they command. He learns to avoid those kinds of self-expression which are not received with gratification and which are therefore less gratifying to him.

If we concentrate for long enough on the therapy of small interacting groups we may notice all of these things happening at different times to different people.

Ottaway offers the recording from Mrs 'P' where she shows explicitly her need to relive her childhood situation and to reenact her attitudes to her father and her brother by transference to members of the group:[16]

> There is a similarity between Mr. J. and Mr. N.—note their clash within the group. Whereas at first I have seen in Mr. N. only my younger brother I only just realised that he (my brother) was the favourite of my father, i.e. like my father. Mr. N's and my brother's character are however more tolerable as they occasionally admit to having bad feelings. That's when I liked Mr. N. My subconscious desire was to be liked by him, as I wanted to be liked by my father, and my bewildered feelings that I could feel hostile, even cruel towards Mr. N.

Elsewhere, the participant may not be as self-conscious or as analytical of the therapy, although the spectator sees it no less clearly. To quote Dr Button:[17]

> The atmosphere was tense but sympathetic and supportive. Brian addressed a linking question to Andy who responded by talking quite out of context, about his disability and what he obviously considered a disfigurement, and the difficulty it gave him in meeting other people. He stumbled through his statement and I had the impression that he had never before stated this clearly even to himself. The response of the group was very sensitive and supportive.

There can be no exact instructions for those who want to encourage the therapeutic processes of a group. A few evident general principles can be described. We may have to begin with our own quiet example since this may be the only contribution that can be made to acceptance and support for the maladjusted in the group. From time to time, we can appropriately make comments that will help us all to become aware of the feelings of the group and to come to terms with them. We can re-interpret what is misunderstood, 'take down the temperature on occasions', use our own experience to encourage others to be more open, reduce the threatening aspect of the group for the more vulnerable members and moderate the humiliation of those who suddenly feel that they have revealed more of themselves than they should. We can help the strong not to laugh at the weak by suggesting that there is no large divide between them and the most isolated. For the rest, we can improve our skill, not merely with practice, but by acquiring a 'feel' for the office by reading accounts of how others with the same intentions have operated.[18]

(4) Perhaps in stressing the supportive role of the worker and the group in emotional therapy, we have not made it clear that both have a truth-function as well as a love-function. We should be concerned not merely to communicate acceptance whatever the 'isolate' does—which is the first and basic responsibility—but also not to miss realistic opportunities of encouraging him to face the problems in his life that he can do something about.

Among writers in this genre, it is Dr Button who has brought out the point most clearly, almost, one suspects, at times to the extent of being slightly abrasive.[19]

This was the last official session that the group would be together, and I was surprised that Jennifer had said nothing for about half-an-hour. I drew the attention of the group to this, and when they turned to her she said, 'Well, yes, I did want to say something really, but the longer I left it the more difficult it was to get in.' The group was a little shocked at their insensibility.

A. K. Rice, with prolonged experience in these matters, admits that students on his courses may find the situation too stressful but 'to avoid problems in human relationships is often as damaging to those relationships as to try, however ineptly, to solve them'.[20] Although group therapy has not fulfilled all the early expectations that it aroused, the method does seem to work best with the shy and withdrawn.

F Groups in conflict

There frequently occur for us a set of circumstances marked by three distinct features.
(a) We are concerned with the relationship of our association with another association; in other words, with inter-group connections as well as intra-group connections.
(b) There is some conflict of aims and/or methods and/or out-look between the two associations. This is so frequent that it has come to have a technical phrase of its own—'the interface con-frontation'.
(c) Yet it is required in the interest of all, that these two groups, not only effect at least a partial reconciliation, but in one area at least, plan integrated action. And, in the circumstances we are describing, the worker has a responsibility to help along the acceptance of, and planning for, this integrated action.
Perhaps it is as well to pause at this point and decide in more detail what is meant by 'integrated action'. If two groups are in conflict, yet must still live and work together, and so need, to some extent, to resolve the conflict (they cannot, that is, settle the matter by simply ignoring the other), then, broadly speaking, only three courses of action are open to them:
(a) One side may impose its will on the other by sanctions of some kind—physical violence, economic threats or emotional blackmail. Everyone accepts the course of action by the most powerful.

The results of this type of solution are not normally encouraging; the vanquished may obey because they have to, but grudgingly, unwillingly and nourishing thoughts of revenge.

(b) As they cannot reach agreement between themselves, an outside party may be called in to act in some sense as arbitrator, with a mutual agreement that his decision will be accepted. The result may be a complete victory for either side or a compromise with both giving up something at the dictation of the arbitrator. This may be an inevitable solution, given the circumstances, but it can leave behind disappointment and frustration and further conflict may break out.

(c) Integration is usually far more difficult although the rewards are tempting. To quote Haiman: 'It is a process in which we attempt, through discussion, to work out an agreement (not a compromise) which incorporates the thinking of all parties to the dispute—a solution or product of co-operative effort with which they are all satisfied.'[21]

A prison official who runs a counselling group may well find himself caught in cross-fire from both colleagues and prisoners. The former may consider that he is being unrealistic and wasting his time in hoping to gain a response with such methods from such a constituency; the latter may consider it is merely another device to turn them all into stool pigeons. How does he operate to interpret each side to the other, to help them to feel that they can both gain from the operation and to make it contribute to the effective running of the establishment?[22]

A vicar appointed to a new parish discovered there was a deep rift between the younger and older members of the parish which was symbolized by the age-group formation of the congregation at the Sunday services. Yet both groups belonged to the same organization and professed the same faith. What can the vicar do that will help them to undertake together necessary, integrated programmes?

We are familiar with the dilemma in industrial disputes; the 'man in the middle' is often the government official or chosen conciliation officer who seeks to mediate between the two interests. 'Community work' is providing us with many more examples. Often the 'grass-roots community worker' finds himself in the middle of contending lobbies and organizations. He may even have to lead a demonstration against his employers—a specialized aspect of inter-group functioning. T. R. Batten has provided us with a vast collection of casework material which demonstrates again and again this need for skill in forwarding the process of the integration of inter-group co-operation.[23]

Only an unbelievably naïve counsellor would suggest that there is a method constituting at the same time a panacea for inter-group conflict and a policy for integrated action. The issues of the conflict may be too deep and real to be settled. The value systems may represent an uncrossable chasm between the two parties. There may be no feasible area of integrating action. One evening in Jerusalem I sat through a long evening's encounter whilst an Israeli government official in the Department of Education tried to convince a leading Arab youth worker to persuade his units to co-operate in state programmes in the occupied territories; but the project was hopeless from the beginning and perhaps ought not to have been attempted.

But not all conflicting inter-group relations calling for integration are quite as hopeless from the beginning. And there are one or two clear approaches open to the group operative which may offer a chance of success.

(a) In the confrontation he can often intervene in a way that makes the expression of disagreement less sterile. He may do this:

(i) by, in various ways, making clear to both sides what is really being said, what is involved. Part of the clash may be about evidence and part about the different values; at least he can bring this into the open;

(ii) by making sure that the full meaning of what each side asserts is exposed and accepted by the other. Often after a confrontation, two different and garbled versions of what was said or implied are related to outside agencies;

(iii) by seizing every natural opportunity to minimize the consequences of super-charged emotions. He may, for example, suggest an adjournment at a tense moment which allows a cooling-off period. A touch of humour may help.

(b) He can communicate to each party that he sees their point of view although this doesn't necessarily mean he will take their side. 'If I were in your position, I think I should now be saying what you are saying.'

(c) He can seize natural opportunities for presenting the other side in a more favourable light. (Of course, in doing this, he may draw some of the hostility on to his own head, but that need not be a bad thing.) Two things are involved here. Sometimes when two parties quarrel, they are disposed to carry their rejection to the point where they can literally see nothing good in the other side. They put horns on the heads of their opponents. So in industrial disputes, for some, the employers become 'greedy, grasping capitalists' and workers, 'Communistic agitators'. In generational conflict, the old may be identified by the young as 'totally out of touch'; and the young by the old as 'totally irresponsible'. There may be a chance for the worker usefully to expose this emotional irrationality since, in this strange world, few people are wholly bad. The second point suggests that there are grounds for believing that this suggestion is not as naïve as may appear: for conflict between human groups is seldom absolute (neither for that matter is co-operation).

Two football teams are in competition for the same prize of victory; but in wide areas they need to co-operate in order to compete. The captains shake hands before the match; they keep the same rules; they share an ethos.

Illustrations from politics are spectacular. The Berlin Wall was built in August 1961 effectively sealing off the two parts of the city; but not quite. All the time there have continued necessary areas of co-operation, as, for example, about the S-Bahn. On the south-east shore of Galilee is the 'Ein Gev' kibbutz which before the Six Days' War was within the gun-sites of a detachment of Syrian soldiers on a nearby hill. There were frequent incidents during which Israelis were shot in the fields on the slopes of the hill. But there were some occasions at least when members of the Syrian gun crew were invited to the concerts held in the magnificent hall of the kibbutz. And there was another period when the Israelis sent messages like, 'You will see the lights of lots of vehicles tonight along the roads around the kibbutz. It is not manœuvres or the beginning of an attack. We are having a big concert and there will be many visitors.'

Like individuals, groups usually have a love-hate relationship. The opposite of 'love' is not 'hate' but 'indifference'. And the perceptive group worker can often expose the areas of acceptance in a landscape that appears to be dominated by rejection.

(d) By prompting the contenders to identify super-ordinate threats, but even more positively—super-ordinate goals and tasks. Sometimes it does help to point out, 'But if this goes through we shall both suffer' and 'We shall be gobbled up by our competitors.'

A crisis may reveal that men who are deeply divided will be brought together by what imperils all. A Midlands car factory had a record of industrial troubles but when one day, the factory caught fire, management and men risked their lives in a combined effort to tow valuable products to safety.

There have been times when disputants have hailed with joy the offer of a super-ordinate goal. The vicar mentioned earlier went some way to healing the breach between young and old by a scheme which involved both in a campaign to collect money for Oxfam. The warden of a community centre, also faced with generational conflict, had all ages uniting in the organization of a series of lavish parties. The common aspiration and endeavour may arise from the conflict itself; this, ideally, is what 'productivity deals' try to achieve in industrial disputes. Or, as in the case of the vicar, it may be better to turn away from the conflict, and seek the unifying project in a new place.

G Groups for social education

We are concerned here with those groups whose prime objective is social education. This means that it does not give priority to the acquisition of knowledge or of a vocational skill. The association aims to help people to find their true place in the community, make good personal and group relationships, accept the responsibility of being a citizen and gain the provided resources for work, leisure and family life. This is what youth service in this country seeks to be.[24] The main aim is no longer, as in the nineteenth century, to give basic education to the 'unschooled' or to provide the economic necessities of life for the deprived—but to encourage social education among youngsters who may find our fast-changing world complex and confusing.

This will be a short section for two reasons. First, this is a sphere where the general principles we have outlined earlier in this chapter have the widest application. Second, this is a subject on which many recent books have been written and an economical use of our time is to make reference here to some of them.[25]

One or two features of group skills in this setting justify brief treatment here.

(a) The process of social education is facilitated by the provision of experiences more frequently than by talking about it. A truly democratic organizational way of running a youth club is more eloquent than a lecture on the subject. Voluntary community work by young people should grow out of visits to places of need rather than from appeals by an older person. Wise social education provides the raw material for decisions, but does not try to force the decisions.

> As a Christian Youth Worker, I feel I have some responsibility for the religious education of our members. Honestly, I don't want to push religion down their throats; and I would certainly not have any compulsory religious activity in the club. But I think they ought to be presented with a good statement of the Christian case; even if they go on to reject it. Well, accordingly, after consultation with the members' committee, I arranged a voluntary epilogue at the end of the evening. But very few came. In the end we had to drop it. Then I had another idea. I suggested we went for a day's outing to Coventry and included a visit to the Cathedral. I never attempted any comment but the burnt cross in the ruins and the international centre, as well as the massive splendour of the new building made many of them think. They had endless questions afterwards about faith and so on. We haven't repeated the Epilogue but a discussion of religious questions is now much more natural for many of our members.

(b) Paternalism is to be eschewed; it is in fact no more than authoritarianism with a conscience. Perish the thought that the social educators of the young should be over-protective. Yet the fact remains that because of their stage of emotional and social development they are often discovered to be in need of encouragement and counselling, if they are to have the confidence to gain from the group. For example, they are frequently very susceptible to praise and can do far more in a climate of appreciation. They constitute one of the examples (if the simile is not misunderstood) of the necessity of the group worker sometimes to give individual 'feeding' to members.

> Mary stayed behind after club last night to see me. She is treasurer and had to hand over some monies. But as she hung about, it became clear to me that there was something else she wanted to talk about. At last it came out. Ken, the chairman, had criticized her rather sharply for not being at the last meeting of the committee. I tried to get her to see this in perspective;

but when it seemed right, I said to her, 'You sometimes give me the impression that you don't care very much about things.' And then it came out. This was a front she put up; behind it she felt completely lacking in self-confidence, mostly because all her brothers and sisters were much cleverer than she was.

(c) Social educational programmes, especially for young adults, should contain possibilities for the participants of learning to exercise their own organizational skills so that they may gain for themselves and their peers what they need in their community. Two of the most recent research projects about adolescents in Britain independently stressed this requirement. In one, John Leigh[26] wrote about youngsters in Derbyshire who can be described as 'leisure-deprived' since there is a meagre provision of available facilities for their off-duty hours; but they also lack the skill and the confidence to employ what there is. In the other,[27] after a prolonged investigation into the attitudes of adolescents to adult authority, the author stresses the same obligation for youthful training in organizational skills.

The place of role-playing

Readers who are familiar with this subject may be surprised that thus far, in a chapter on 'Action', nothing has been said about role-playing. There is a reason. This technique can be very valuable, but it is hedged about with hazards and limitations. Hence the decision to treat it separately at the end of the chapter. This should not obscure the fact that role-playing approaches under certain circumstances might be relevant to working out some of the situations which we have already described; having read this section the reader may care to look back with this in mind.

As the sociologists have lavishly demonstrated, we all of us play roles throughout our daily lives. But in the present discourse, 'role-playing' has a different connotation. It means the rehearsal of situations for purposes of play, elucidation, training or insight. So children indulge in this pastime and it is probably nature's way of preparing them for adulthood. 'I'll be mother. Tommy can be the Doctor. This is my baby [holding up her doll]. Jane is the Nurse and John is Daddy.' Readers of detective fiction are familiar with the method—dear to the heart of Hercules Poirot—whereby the sleuth reconstructs the crime, with a full dramatic cast; the belief being that in this way a vital clue may reveal itself. But we are more closely concerned with two further uses which often overlap.

One is as a device for training where attempting something at one level prepares us to do it better at a higher and possibly the real level. The golfer essays a practice putt before striking the ball. Police cadets are given simple police duties before they become fully-fledged members of the force. The other purpose is to help the participants to understand the feelings of people who might be involved in those circumstances just as, for example, an actor might say that he never understood what it meant to be a homosexual in our society until he had played the part of a homosexual in a film or play. Perhaps we can increase this second purpose to include helping us to understand better the human situation in which we ourselves are involved, widening our knowledge and experience, realizing more of our possibilities, releasing our inhibitions and helping us to establish happier relationships with our fellows, as well as working out problems.

The method works, as I can testify, along with many others. Role-playing techniques can be a useful training method for professional roles; it can help us understand what is happening to others when we dramatize their experience; it can even be a way of perceiving answers to riddles that have baffled us.[28]

But it is a method that requires careful use or it can be not only futile, but even dangerous; hence, the offer of the following principles.

(1) The exercise calls for the most meticulous preparation; everybody taking part as 'actors' or observers and assessors must be crystal clear what this particular exercise is about, and what it aims to do. Many role-playing sessions are doomed to failure from the beginning because of faulty and incomplete preparation.

(2) To have any chance of success, the session must relate to circumstances in which the participants now find themselves involved, or are likely to be in the near future. It is no use merely saying, 'Let's pretend.' To my knowledge, the most productive role-play arises from the dilemmas of a training-group who have been working together at the understanding of a human situation and getting nowhere. Then the tutor says, 'Let's role-play this case and see if there is anything else we can see.' In my view, without a commitment of this kind the participants are unlikely to make the right mental approach to the enterprise; it must have this

'reality' for them. Otherwise, in the worst cases, it ends up as a charade!

(3) This is one of the places where the group worker usually has to be fairly active and employ an element of control in the choice of cast, in the scene itself, the timing and the assessment. The audience, for example, may lose interest before the actors, who may have talked the subject through and merely gone on repeating themselves.

(4) In a relaxed and friendly manner it may be necessary to use a few mechanisms of protection for one or more of the participants. I usually do this in a general way by making the point very strongly at the beginning that when we come to assess, we are not criticizing the actor as a performer or a person, but the role that he played. Otherwise, we would expect Boris Karloff to be an unpleasant person in private life! This is all the more necessary because many role-playing sessions are successful to the degree that people become so involved that they forget that we have made it up! Even so, it is important for the group worker to reserve a sharp eye for the participant who becomes too involved emotionally or loses control of himself.

(5) In the subsequent assessment, we want to discover what all this means, what we have learned and felt. There is no one time sequence or order; but (1) we should aim to involve both actors and audience; (2) keep the purpose clear; (3) assess the total exercise (was the whole ground covered? Were the issues fairly discussed?); (4) assess each role; (5) decide what we have learned; (6) ask whether any general principle in our work is suggested by the enterprise.

Leadership

In the preceding pages many references have been made to leadership, its appropriate skills and different types and styles. The subject is crucial to our whole study. In practice, many students fail to make satisfactory progress until they come to terms with the notion of leadership and apply their discoveries to themselves. A change of mind in this area can sometimes mean a change of heart. 'Through this course of study, I came to realise that for years I had been working as an authoritarian leader, always knowing what was best for people. Now I use entirely different methods.' That was said recently by a minister of religion who had spent many years virtually as a community worker in neighbourhoods with a high quota of 'immigrants'. In religious language, which he would appreciate but which we would not want to press too far here, thinking in a group about the meaning of leadership had been a 'Damascus Road' encounter for him. Again and again, I have noticed that it has been determinative for the progress of students learning group skill. And that is why it is the connecting thread in the pages that have gone before.

It will not have escaped the attention of the perceptive reader that we have frequently failed to distinguish between two orientations of leadership—that which aims at achievement and that whose goal is training. A man who is at the head of a mountaineering expedition may be considered to have a vastly different task than a tutor on a social work course concerned with the development of skill and insight among a class of students. Yet the failure to distinguish is not accidental. It rests on the conviction that there should be no dichotomy between task and training. After all, we are concerned with social group method which means that however large the task content of the association, we are at least as concerned with the personal and social development of the participants. More concretely we may affirm that every task-orientated group is concerned with training in personal and social development and every training group has a better chance of success if they work together at some task.

As to the first, a good captain of a county cricket team, although primarily concerned with success on the field, realizes that he is a group worker with the team, although he may not use the title;

apart from their growing prowess with bat and ball, they are in a training situation because they need to learn sensitivity to each other in personal relationships. As to the second, a tutor has a better chance of success if he meets the students, not only in the lecture room, but shares a project—of research or community work—with them. Task and training cannot be separated; their close association here is deliberate and inevitable. In the view of the present writer, it is the failure to recognize this simple reality which weakens both many pieces of community work (where the ongoing training factor is neglected) and many training courses (where the training is offered, so to speak, 'in a vacuum', away from the human structure with which the students will be professionally concerned).

So the time has come in the concluding chapter to draw together the scattered threads of our thinking about leadership. We can gain further understanding by a brief glance at what has been said on the subject by philosophers, sociologists and social psychologists who have specialized in this field. By this means, we may sort out our ideas and produce a more systematic consideration than has been possible so far. In pubs and other places where people often engage in serious conversation and explore the real issues of existence, the subject of leadership is not entirely neglected; it is in fact a subject of fairly general concern. And the conversationalists have a habit of reaching the heart of the matter although they probably use language that would not come naturally to a professional psychologist. But they are likely in their own way to explore the issues which have preoccupied the academics; and, in particular, on this issue they quickly reach the point where they are discussing whether leaders are born or made. Do leaders create situations or are leaders fashioned by the situations they confront? I have listened to and taken part in many conversations about these fundamental issues among people who would not regard themselves as well educated.

It is true, of course, that many such conversations are not always pursued to their logical conclusion; and the relaxed atmosphere in which they take place may be an inhibiting factor in this regard. Students, however, have a duty to make a more rigorous examination and at least to avoid one or two of the absurdities by which we may be betrayed. To ask whether Hitler created the 'German problem' or whether the 'German problem' was in the end bound to produce a Hitler, is manifestly ridiculous if we assume that there is an answer which absolutely locates the cause either in the personality of an evil genius or in the prevailing cultural factors. At the first session of a weekend training course, one of the students made a short speech in which he sought emphatically to drive home two points which were for him deeply-held convictions. 'Leaders are born not made.' 'Human nature can't be changed.' If he was right on both points it was difficult to understand why he had bothered to enrol for the course.

Students have a duty then to think logically about the subject of leadership; it is also incumbent upon them to take account of, and have their thinking chastened by, the deliberations of some of the scholars who have devoted time and attention to the subject.

They quickly discover that there has been a Copernican revolution in this realm; the balance in the understanding and conceptualization of leadership has passed from an emphasis on character traits to an emphasis on situations.

The older tradition held sway for a long time; its advocates include notable and eloquent persuaders like Plutarch and Carlyle; its basic position is that leaders are innately different from followers; they are 'born to rule' because they have certain inherited characteristics. Moreover, the emphasis is often pressed to the point where these natural leaders are expected to be successful in every type of situation where they are called upon to influence the behaviour of other people, so that—to parody the position—the leadership qualities are the same for a pastor and a sergeant-major.

It is Carlyle who, in a robust, knock-about style, expresses most strongly the view that leaders are not the product of cultural determinism, but are unpredictable, 'gifts from the gods', giants with magical powers:[1]

Show our critics a great man, a Luther for example, they begin to what they call 'account' for him ... and bring him out to be a little kind of man. He was the 'creature of the Time' they say; the Time called him forth, the Time did everything, he nothing. ... Alas, we have known times call loudly enough for their Great Men but not find them when they call. He was not there, Providence had not sent him; the Time, calling its loudest, had to go down to confusion and wreck because he would not come when called. ... In all epochs of the World's history we shall find the Great Man to have been the

indispensable saviour of his epoch; the lightning, without
which the fuel would never have been burnt.

Perhaps Carlyle's supernatural references are not always to be
taken literally, although behind many of the old approaches there
was a belief in supernatural endowments which might be loans
from the devil as well as 'gifts from the gods' or connected with
magical circumstances associated with conception. But more commonly today, the interpretation of leadership primarily by
character traits is content to deal in unusual gifts without speculating about their origin—tirelessness, quickness of decision, intuition. So long as this approach held sway, we were content to study
leadership in the biography of great men, through experiments to
identify the personal qualities that influence behaviour and by
looking carefully at leaders in action.

That the interpretation led the field for so long suggests that it
cannot be totally false-based as it would be on close and prolonged
observation of human interaction. And the notion that leaders are
'born not made' receives some confirmation in our common
observation of the human scene. In fact, many social psychologists
are not concerned to deny the influence of traits in leadership but
to minimize their importance in our assessment, not to allow them
to fill the whole picture, as their custom has been. Thrasher
discovered that gameness, physical prowess, speed and finality of
decision were the commonest qualities associated with leadership
in boys' gangs.[2] Another study in our period found that other
things being equal, in American society, those who were above
average height and weight, and were attractive in appearance,
stood a better chance of being chosen as leaders.[3] Predictably, in
the same culture, it has also been pointed out that, on the whole,
those who talk more in groups are likely to be wanted for leadership.

For our purpose, it is enough to point out that the 'revolution',
to which we referred, is a change of emphasis rather than a complete refutation of what has gone before.[4] Despite vastly improved
techniques for measuring traits, the whole assumption has been
questioned on the grounds that it makes value-judgments which
are not validated, but, even more pertinently for our purpose, that
it fails to take sufficient account of the characteristics of the
situation. To quote Bavelas:[5]

There is a second and more interesting objection that has been
made to the trait approach. It is based not on the question of the

accuracy or the validity of the assumptions that are made but upon the nature of the 'traits' themselves. Traits are, after all, statements about personal characteristics. The objection to this is that the degree to which an individual exhibits leadership depends not only upon his characteristics but, also, on the characteristics of the situation in which he finds himself. . . .
In these terms we come close to the notion of leadership, not as a personal quality, but as an organisational function.

A few students find a study of modern concepts of leadership rewarding both for their own personal development and academic progress. (As with much else in sociology, some of the seminal ideas are to be found in Weber but we need to push on to later conclusions based on research specifically devoted to this concern.) But the constant hope is that they will integrate their new insights with professional practice because they grasp that their influence is based on the interaction of personality and situations; that although they are called to use the gifts they have, it must be in a way that is patterned partly by the role-expectations of those among whom they work. In this territory lie many of the useful discussions which usually take place towards the beginning of the course. If the tutor were to anticipate and telescope what he hopes they will find for themselves through group interaction, study and supervised practice, he would say:

'There are many different types and styles of leadership.'
'Yours will be conditioned by the kind of person you are which in turn will have been conditioned by the kind of social experiences you have had.'
'But as you go on your style and methods should be modified by the demands of the situation in which you find yourself, the nearer and more remote environment in which you operate, the needs of the people among whom you work.'

In point of fact, it would be most unprofessional for a tutor to make a statement like that. If these propositions are true they have to be experienced by the students; to have any power they cannot be presented on a plate as the fruit of another's reflections.
Another pursuit is found in practice often to stimulate intellectual curiosity and contribute to the student's general progress; that is, to enquire why the 'break through' has come at this time. Changes of this kind are not fortuitous; they are nearly always

found to be related to the cultural dynamics of our age. The new emphasis cannot be entirely explained in terms of the new psychological knowledge which is ours, notably our better grasp of the social nature of personality. It seems to arise from the unconscious, from the emotional depths of many twentieth-century men, as well as from the conscious, the rational analysis. Karl Mannheim made us familiar with the notion of 'the sociology of knowledge'; the views that we hold, the knowledge we have, are part of our adaptation to the environment and are functional for our existence.[6] Clearly this interpretation applies to the present topic.

The disastrous example of modern political dictators has succeeded in making 'leader' a dirty word for many people in the western world. There may have been for some intellectuals an attraction about the *Führer Prinzip* until they saw the results in practice. Would Carlyle revise his views in the light of twentieth-century events? The terms 'democratic' and 'authoritarian' applied to the leadership have nearly passed into common speech. The monumental work by Adorno, Frenkel-Brunswick, Levinson and Sandford on the personality type indicated describes the black angels of twentieth-century imagination.[7] It is almost with a shudder at the memory of the dark deeds of charismatic leaders that we have turned to a situational interpretation of leadership.

Positively, in Britain at least, there has been a marked growth in the sentiment that the individual member of society—irrespective of rank or position—is important; he should be cared for, his views taken into account and his talents not neglected or unacknowledged. The statement made in private conversation or public meeting is calculated to evoke a swift objection that neither the process of democratization nor our social policies reflect the sentiment so far. Yet clearly our political structure, our educational system and our welfare programmes have not been unaffected by the notion.

More pertinently, the old notions of our dependence upon the few, specially-gifted leaders could not live in the rarefied atmosphere that we breathe today; and on examination, many of the old views are seen to rest on a philosophy of profound contempt for the masses. From Aristotle through to Augustus and Machiavelli, and to some extent Lenin, there is a reliance, to a degree, on the assumption of mindless masses and strong-willed leaders. And, of course, it was a self-fulfilling prophecy; so long as everybody

believed this to be true it was so. Le Bon too worked on the
assumption of the drifting mob and the purposeful leader. In his
case, he made his thesis explicit: the majority of men do not possess
clear and reasoned ideas on any subject whatever outside their own
specialism. The old approach is quite alien to the spirit of the age—
in Britain at least. Whatever justification there is for their optimism,
most articulate citizens today are openly dedicated to the proposition that the community has a responsibility to the individual—
to protect and support him, but also to respect him. The current
mood was bound to affect the way we think about leadership.[8] We
may even be disposed to agree that 'leaders are born not made';
but inwardly, we are much more likely today to add the corollary
that far more of them are born than is commonly supposed; that
the talent for leadership is not restricted to one social class or one
type of education; and the great pity is that many of them never
have the opportunity to develop and display their gifts.[9] The old
world concluded: 'We cannot all be masters';[10] we are more
impressed by the fact that—as Thomas Gray says:

> Some village—Hampden, that with dauntless breast
> The little tyrant of his fields withstood;
> Some mute inglorious Milton here may rest,
> Some Cromwell guiltless of his country's blood
> > (*Elegy. Written in a Country Churchyard*).

Among large sections of the population in this country there is a
deepening conviction that the ruling classes, a minority, have for
too long sustained a vast confidence trick to exercise control over
the majority. But these days are over; the bluff has been called;
for the masses it is no longer a question of 'theirs not to reason
why'; almost every form of authority is called into question. One
of the revealing presentations of recent years has been the film
Oh What a Lovely War. At the church parade, the soldiers sing
their own version to the tune of 'What a friend we have in Jesus',
thereby rejecting at one stroke the ancient authority of both church
and state:

> When this lousy War is over
> No more church parades for me . . .

But the rejection is more than a sentiment in the minds of man; it
passes into action; in the post-war period the masses have become
conscious of their power; more and more of the mechanisms of

social control have to be adjusted, revised or scrapped; more and more, successive governments have to learn how to govern with the consent of the governed. Workers will not allow their factories to be closed by decisions from above. Laws can be broken with impunity by powerful minority groups. Popular demonstrations can keep the South African cricket team at home, change the siting of an airport, alter the direction of a major road or establish an official road-crossing near a school.

To see the reality of the transfer of power at its most dramatic, however, we have to go to Calcutta—a city of such poignant human need that a few days' visit can be traumatic for a European with any humanity and sensitivity.[11] Thousands have their only home on the pavements, perhaps below brilliantly-illuminated hoardings which invite them to purchase expensive mattresses. There are nearly forty-thousand lepers in the city. On the west side of the Hoogley River live half-a-million people without a covered drain between them. When I visited the chief planning officer in his room, he greeted me with the words, 'You have come to a dying city.' Slogans on walls read: 'No hope left. Only anger.'

Not surprisingly, it is in this city that a technique of protest has been developed—called 'gherao'—which mobilizes the only resource within reach of the masses—the sheer weight of numbers. In industrial action, an employer who refuses to yield to the demands of the workers will, when he goes out to get into his car, simply be surrounded in the yard of his factory by a crowd who will not molest him but simply imprison him there and the combined effects of fear, suffocation, thirst and hunger will force him to yield to their demands. Geoffrey Moorhouse comments:

> Men have collapsed half-dead from exhaustion and de-hydration in Calcutta after being gheraoed in the blazing sun for the best part of a day by perpetually fresh mobs operating a shift system [p. 201]. . . . The manager of a factory just behind Park Street was forced to stand in the sun for seven hours without any water and without being allowed to use the lavatory, while the girl on the switchboard was threatened with violence if she tried to call the Police [p. 313].

Moorhouse wonders if the ultimate fate of Calcutta will not be decided by a massive 'gherao' seeking a final solution. 'The arsenals of the rich will be no protection against this onslaught in the close confinements of Calcutta, for there are so many millions of poor here and only a few thousand of rich, and life is very cheaply lived upon a pavement and in a bustee.'[12] In the sharply contrasted conditions of developed countries—whose poorest live like princes compared with the beggars of Calcutta—we have our own much milder form of 'gherao'; the masses are more aware of their power today and they are beginning to use it.

This digression is not doctrinaire; those, including group workers, who wish to influence the behaviour of their fellows, have to try to grasp the total situation in which they operate. Part of that total situation is the psychological climate which is beginning to think and to act on the conviction that Jack is at least as good as his master, and far more powerful in association. The insistence that leadership shall be understood situationally springs not from the erudite reporting of scholars and researchers alone; it is powerfully reinforced by the subconscious assumptions of our time.

Consequences for group workers

The new approaches do not go unchallenged; changes usually produce a backlash. And although the tide is running strongly in favour of democratization, there are strong eddies from time to time flowing in a contrary direction. We may have an epidemic of editorials in the popular press on the general theme, 'What this country needs is strong leadership.' A not infrequent phrase which is used in social conversations is: 'There must always be masters and men.'

At a more thoughtful level, psychologists point to the presence in the human psyche of a drive to submission as well as to dominance. (Although they do not always come to terms with the dilemma of deciding how much of this is inherited from our cultural past; perhaps the need for dependence is less pronounced in a modern egalitarian society.) At a generalized theoretical level, Kimball Young[13] has argued that dominance and submission are facts of most animal existence: 'Forms as low as lizards develop a hierarchy of dominance and submission in which a stronger and older member comes to control over other members of the species within a certain area' [p. 222].

In a work for popular consumption, Vance Packard reports that his interest in human stratification systems was first aroused when his father, a farmer in Pennsylvania, pointed out that there was one cow, Gertrude, who always came first through the gate at feeding time and another rather runty cow who always came last. Much later in his life, the trainer of the world-famous chimpanzees at St Louis told him of his methods:[14]

> First I stand back and watch a new group for a while to see who is going to be boss. Once that is settled I have little difficulty. The boss chimp, when I get him on my side, keeps the rest of them in line. They are more scared of him than they are of me.

That there is a pecking order in the world of animals, and that this extends to most human groups, is a conviction which is shared by professional psychologists and the general public.[15]

None of this need make us hesitate as group workers to focus our attention on the factors in leadership which arise from the situation rather than from the personality factors of the people concerned. In doing this we are merely redressing the claim of the centuries in a favourable moral climate. Moreover, since the indigenous realities of leadership are present and recognized, they can usually be allowed to make their own presence felt; whereas it is often required to seek for the situational effects; they speak with softer voices and are often unheard.

But that they are there more than ever in our age is demonstrated in two unexpected places. Most people would not violently disagree with the statement that the army and the police force—for reasons that could be regarded as sufficient—are among the most authoritarian and rigidly structured systems in our society. There is a clear hierarchy of rank with unmistakable symbols; orders come down from above and are not normally questioned. Yet both in recent years have made significant gestures in the direction of recognizing that leadership—both internal and external—must go some way to recognizing the role-expectations of those who receive orders, that rule must seek the consent of those who are ruled. Police cadet-training includes community work among its programmes. As for the army, a great deal is made of this point by Field-Marshal Montgomery in his autobiography, a man who could hardly be regarded as the least authoritarian figure of his generation.[16]

> Bottled up in men are great emotional forces which have got to be given an outlet in a way which is positive and constructive, and which warms the heart and excites the imagination [p. 83].

Every single soldier must know before he goes into battle, how the little battle he is to fight fits into the larger picture, and how the success of his fighting will influence the battle as a whole [p. 88].

It must be realized that these men are very different from the soldiers and sailors of the Boer War era, or even of the 1914 period. The young man of today reads the newspapers. . . . He is daily taking in information and relating it to himself. He can think, he can appreciate, and he is definitely prepared to criticize. He wants to know what is going on, and what you want him to do—and why and when [p. 89].

Anyone who considers Montgomery to represent a minimal concession to democratization, should consider Wellington's attitude to his soldiers a century and a quarter earlier:[17]

The conscription calls out a share of every class—no matter whether your son or my son; but our friends [the British Army composed of volunteers]—I may say it in this room—are the very scum of the earth. People talk of their enlisting from fine military feeling—all stuff—no such thing. Some of our men enlist from having got bastard children—some for minor offences—many more for drink; but you can hardly conceive such a set brought together, and it really is wonderful that we should have made them the fine fellows they are.

In my view a long preoccupation with the concept of leadership on a training course for group workers is justified on several grounds, even apart from its primary and practical purpose in stimulating the student to be more reflective and analytical about his own style and method. The fact is that for many students it is the entrance gate to sociological study and perspective. Sociology is one of those subjects which the student is unlikely to have attempted at school, and therefore he is not familiar with its disciplined way of looking at the human scene. It is like learning a new language and the tutor is all the time searching for teaching models and methods.

On the courses with which I have been most concerned over the past decade, I have become familiar with the mature student whose intellectual potential has never been discovered by the community or realized by himself in twentieth-century Britain; a sad figure who has slipped through all our educational nets. And I have found that to a significant minority of these students, a study of leadership offers the possibility of an exciting intellectual adventure which often proves determinative for their academic confidence. There seems to be something about the subject which makes it peculiarly fitting for this purpose. Perhaps it is partly because although there is a whole body of accumulated knowledge on the topic, it begins in their own experience; all their lives they have known leaders of one sort or another. It proves to be an illuminating subject, a liberal study, in the sense that as we go on, it helps us to understand, analyse and interpret our own experience of life. Apart from this, it is a fascinating subject in its own right as the following illustrations may demonstrate.

There are famous distinctions like Arthur Koestler's identification of the 'yogi' and the 'commissar'. We cannot fail to recognize both types. The yogi is contemplative, a man of ideas; but he cannot organize anything. He is a disaster as an administrator, and if the organization can afford the indulgence, he should be paid to sit in a room and think. By contrast, the commissar is a man of action; he is capable for years of being an efficient cog in a machine without ever asking any basic questions about the finished product or whether there could be radical changes in the whole operation. Of course, these are ideal types in the Weberian sense, overdrawn to make a point stand out; perhaps nobody is one hundred per cent yogi or commissar. But they do afford insight into many leadership situations. Few school or college staffs or business organizations are without members who show a marked preference for one or other of these styles.

Antony Jay has written a book[18] about leaders in business which has the singular merit of being as amusing as it is informative:

> Richard Coeur de Lion was one of those managers who was first-rate at his own job but never grew up with the wider responsibilities of managing the whole business [pp. 135-6] ... there is a kind of leader who manages to see only the tiny crumbs of comfort and ignores and shuts himself off from all the signs of approaching disaster. Nicholas II, with the invaluable assistance of his wife, managed to build himself a fantasy world which he inhabited up to 1917. You would have thought the signs were unmistakable but he managed to mistake them and reassure himself with trivia [pp. 136-7].

There is profit also in referring to various attempts to construct typologies of leadership so long as we do not fall into what I have found a common error among students and press the theories further than they were ever intended to go, imposing them rigidly upon every leadership situation we assess. But as aids to insight they can often prove useful. For example, there is Ross and Hendry's scheme.[19] They distinguish three types of leadership: (1) the person who has achieved prominence by unique attainment, who is *ahead* of his group; (2) the person who by designation has been given an official status; who is then *the head* of his group; (3) the person who emerges in a given situation in ways the group recognizes as needed, that is one who is *a head* of his group. The typology is not only reminiscent of Weber's famous analysis, but also concentrates on one of the recurring distinctions: that is, between the leader who is appointed from outside, is a formal leader holding an official position and the leader who is elected from inside, is an informal and indigenous leader, there because the group want him to be leader. (And just here lies for students a common transfer from theorizing to a change in practice when they come to terms with the fact—experientially not merely intellectually, where the point is obvious—that in their professional roles they are imposed, appointed leaders, who must gain acceptance in the group.)

Patterns of leadership may also usefully be examined in the light of David Riesman's well-known scheme of social types of personality;[20] here we look at the way leaders perform and estimate from which base they are operating. His three types are: (1) The 'tradition-directed' whose behaviour is controlled by traditional standards expressed through kinship ties, religion, ceremonials and the like; they are the conformists. (2) The 'inner-directed' are more responsive to the goals implanted in them in the family during their early years. (3) By contrast, the 'other-directed' are those for whom their contemporaries are the guide; they follow the crowd.

It is interesting to find the stress on situational factors in John F. Kennedy's well-known book on political leadership, *Profiles in Courage*.[21] His main thesis is that although senators and congressmen should be guided by high principles, they have to remain to a degree representative of their electors' wishes, and this not only to retain popularity and support, but to fulfil their office.

But this is no real problem, some will say. Always do what is right, regardless of whether it is popular. Ignore the pressures, the temptation, the false compromises. That is an easy answer— but it is easy only for those who do not bear the responsibilities of elected office. Far more is involved than pressure politics and personal ambitions. Are we rightfully entitled to ignore the demands of our constituents even if we are able and willing to do so?

From the kind of platform we have been describing in the last few paragraphs—erected on a sound basis of students' interest in the human scene—students are able to proceed to a study that is more demanding academically, in both the psychological and sociological fields.

There is one chapter in a book by Gerth and Wright Mills[22] which a grateful tutor might be forgiven for supposing was tailor-made for this purpose. It offers concepts which often call for swift recognition as 'what we have always felt and known but have never been able to put into words'. The authors point out that there are three aspects of authority or features of leadership. The first is made up of the symbols of the role, as, for example, when the national anthem is played in the presence of the queen, or a civil servant, on promotion, acquires a larger desk, or a citizen mentioned in the Honours List henceforth has the preface 'Sir' attached to his name. The second aspect is the legitimation of the role, the formal doctrines of its authority. An example is the Stuart belief in the divine right of kings. Finally, there is the actual decision-making which can be viewed separately from the first two. A constitutional monarch, for example, could have both the ceremonials and the legitimations of position with little real power.

Gerth and Mills go on to show that the permutations of the three features give us eight types of leadership in society. Napoleon is one of those rare human beings who scores an affirmative in all three aspects; he was emperor and enjoyed the ceremonials of the office; he took care to see that he was crowned by the pope, a visual legitimation of his position; for years, he wielded power. Cromwell, on the other hand, lacked legitimation of his rule.

Closer to our own experience is the authors' discussion of the leadership as role-determined or self-determined. How much flexibility, how much freedom to interpret the role, does any leader have? Of what strength and nature are the pressures brought upon him to act in prescribed ways? So we have: (1) the routinees where the role is defined; (2) the innovators, who, within an existing institution, have some room to personalize their performance; (3) the precursors who create a role for which, when they take over, there is no institution where they can perform it.

From all of this it will be clear that we are resting a lot of weight on the conviction (born during years of tutoring) that a study of leadership can be in several ways rewarding, particularly for the mature student who has not previously enjoyed the advantages of full-time higher education. It can encourage his personal development, prompting a fresh interpretation of his own life as well as often nourishing the roots of his self-confidence for academic work; it can add to his store of knowledge. But time on these courses devoted to this aspect must justify itself in practical work since the primary purpose of the courses is to produce more efficient workers. It is here that we return to what we regard as the signature tune of the modern researcher into the meaning and function of leadership. C. A. Gibb comments:[23]

> Leadership has usually been thought of as a specific attribute of personality, a personality trait that some possess and others do not, or at least that some achieve in high degree and others scarcely at all. The search for leaders has often been directed toward finding those persons who have this trait well developed. The truth however would seem to be quite different. In fact, viewed in relation to the individual, leadership is not an attribute of the personality but a quality of his role within a particular and specified social system. Viewed in relation to the group, leadership is a quality of its structure.

Normally there is a stage in the student's progress when he accepts this principle with, so to speak, the top of his mind; at this time he is prone to write eloquently on this theme in essays. But when through tutorials, supervision and group-discussions, the notion is applied to the way he exercises leadership, he finds the issue is existential; all at once his sensitivity, his motives, his values, his objectivity about himself, come under severe self-scrutiny; in a few extreme cases, his personal world is shaken to its foundations. But even this 'troubling of the waters' can be the prelude to a style of leadership which is not spoiled but is enhanced by being more aware of itself as is demonstrated in the following extract from the recording of a student training to be a residential child care worker and placed in a remand home: 'I assume the maternal role when the housemother has her days off and I think now this was a definite plan on my part.' In other extracts, we see the students estimating the role-performance of those they observed in depth and with sophistication:

> By just being a teacher within a classroom situation the teacher assumes a definite leadership role. There are decisions which he can take and which the pupils cannot. In a therapeutic community the classroom is regarded as 'belonging to all the members'. This does not negate the teacher's leadership role but necessitates a freer exchange between teachers and pupils than is usual. The teacher is still responsible to the principal for the control and education of his class.

Elsewhere, the validity of the 'situation-orientated' approach to the theory and practice of leadership may require considerable modification. There are crises where strong charismatic directions are called for. General Gordon sent a message from Cairo to the besieged community in Khartoum: 'Do not be panic-stricken. You are men not women.' So Vandamme said of Napoleon: 'That devil of a man exercises upon me a fascination that I cannot explain to myself, and in such a degree that, though I fear neither God nor devil, he could make me go through the eye of a needle to throw myself into the fire.' But in the main for the small group, strong charismatic control is dysfunctional. This point is made explicit in many interpretive recordings:

> The warden makes all the decisions concerning the running of the hostel, the admission and treatment of the residents. She delegates little authority to the other staff members and rarely consults them on any matter. They in their turn offer no protest when they disagree with warden's decisions or policy and carry out both without question.

> The principal is a dominator. He fits into discussions that are formal, which allow him the full use of his authority. He avoids critical discussions. In my opinion this is a sign of his weakness and lack of ability to lead a group of mature people, and as such he feels threatened by this possible exposure.

For the small group, enabling rather than dictatorial guidance is nearly always right and we can see at once why this is so. They are face-to-face groupings where a complete network of personal relationships is possible. For the leader, this presents both an opportunity and a hazard. A dictator has more difficulty in establishing personal relationships with members of the group since he lacks the necessary give and take; on the other hand, in so far as he succeeds, the individual member will be more at the mercy of the authoritarian, charismatic leader who has established a personal relationship. There is the related reality that the aim of the small group is almost always educational for its constituency; the process is at least as important as the product. The real harm done by the dominating leader, guided by his character traits rather than by the social situation, is that he prevents the group members from using their own experiences by imposing upon them his own; thus he diverts them from their proper invaluable educational tasks. Another way of putting the same point is to say that his character may inhibit the group's development and employment of its own total resources, which, as we have repeatedly said, is the first goal of group work. To quote Dr Button:[24]

> There are important distinctions between the small group
> worker and the institutional group worker. The latter bears
> responsibility for an establishment as a whole, having within
> it a series of natural and contrived small groups, which may be
> separate from one another or be linked by a complex network
> of relationships. . . . Although it is not always recognised as
> such, there is an important element of institutional group work
> in many people's jobs [but] it could be argued that the
> expression 'group worker' should be reserved for those who use
> their influence self-consciously, and it must be granted that in
> many instances cited the worker may be the victim of social
> forces rather than the architect.

Or, in other words, since the group worker has more power in the small association, it is important that he use his influence professionally rather than unthinkingly and that means for education and not for propaganda, as an enabler not a dictator, being guided by the demands of the setting and not by his own character traits.

In professional circles all this is pushing an open door and dispatching coals to Newcastle; in that milieu one can offer no deadlier insult to a worker than to describe him as 'charismatic'.

So much is it the case that one is often tempted to put the opposing point of view in the hope of preserving a balance in the recognition of pressures. In educational and social work as elsewhere, the pendulum swings wildly between one extreme and its contrary; we are sometimes disposed to climb on the band-waggon whose slogans we grasp imperfectly. For one thing democratic leadership is not such a new notion as some of its modern advocates would have us believe. It is a long time now since Lao Tse wrote, 'The greatest leader is he who seems to follow' (*The Book of Tao*).

Further, we find it necessary to stress on occasions that enabling leadership in small groups is not the same as being passive; advocates who confuse the two may learn to their horror one day that they have presented an alibi to the lazy, slack and listless. *Laissez-faire* leaders do not merit much attention because they do not lead but leave the group entirely to itself and do not participate. Democratic leaders are not to be distinguished by their lack of activity but by the nature and quality of their activity. They do not give orders without consulting the group; they work out acceptable policies with the group; they look for praise, blame and discipline to come from the group rather than from themselves. Another factor which should modify our enthusiasm is that not all the advantages are in favour of democratic guidance. (Most of them are: people are more likely to support policies in whose formulation they have had a major say; they are likely to feel they are being treated with respect; and so on.) Democracy often works far more slowly than dictatorship; it may not be as efficient in the short-term; it can sometimes represent the naked power of the majority, mob-rule, rather than any genuine trend towards a participant society.

The emphasis upon enabling leadership which starts from the group situation and the needs of its members, rather than from one's own personality, has sometimes led people to suppose that they must forget and even suppress their own personality. As in many other movements, the advocates of social group methods have suffered most at the hands of their disciples, some of whom have been happily de-humanizing themselves in what they suppose to be the appropriate response to the 'new teaching'. But effective group work calls not for the loss or diminution of the natural gifts of personality but for their disciplined use for an educational goal.

One of the recent episodes in the BBC 2 series on 'Working with

Youth' was devoted to counselling. The section that was plainly intended to demonstrate 'how to do it' showed a young teacher, who had undergone a course of training, counselling an adolescent boy with a personal problem in his family background. The success of the group worker here was not entirely unrelated to the fact that he had a ready, warm, attractive and obviously genuine smile which immediately conveyed acceptance to the 'client'. Unless tutoring had taught us otherwise, we might deem it superfluous to say that we do not have to be dull in order to be non-directive; there is even a case for the leader supplying inspiration for the members of the group so long as it 'lights the fires' of their imagination and does not encourage them to warm their hands at his fire.

There is no book of rules for democratic leadership. Even a doctrinaire commitment to a philosophy and method which we have been taught on a training course can be a disguised method of relying upon ourselves rather than responding appropriately to the opportunities. Good group leadership, we repeat, is always related to the right amount of intervention. If we try to do too much, they will be tempted to do too little, leaving a major part of their resources unused and failing to profit by their exposure to inadequacy, conflict and challenge. If we do too little they will lack the required support for the mobilization of their resources for effective goal achievement and self-training. Even about non-directive methods there is nothing sacrosanct; the issue is whether we can use directive and non-directive approaches according to whether one or other is demanded by the situation.

Group leaders must come to terms with themselves

The older type leadership commonly proceeded on the serene assumption of its own superiority. No doubt Nicholas II of Russia is an extreme, almost unique, example. When in 1917 the British ambassador in Petrograd ventured to suggest to the Tsar that perhaps he would be well advised to take more account of the wishes of his subjects, Nicholas is reported to have enquired whether the ambassador did not mean that the subjects should take more account of the wishes of the Tsar. But in a modified form the unexamined hypothesis has operated at lower echelons. Pressed to justify the assumption, men of influence might not have lacked a reply.

They could have said that the unquestioned acceptance of their superiority was required for obedience by the followers. 'Theirs not to reason why' could only go unquestioned so long as officers were thought of as belonging to a different and higher breed of men than the soldiers in the ranks. The older type of leaders under pressure might also have argued that a legend of superiority was required for their own self-confidence.

Today this has changed. Particularly in the settings we have in mind, the leader works with and learns with the followers; and he recognizes that his own contribution has to be assessed critically. This at once tests our emotional maturity and offers the chance of a significant improvement in our performance.

As to the first, most of us resist astringent self-knowledge; we want to live with comfortable illusions about ourselves. When interviewing candidates for a course of training for full-time youth and community workers, I ask two questions: 'In your voluntary work in youth organizations, what do you think was your main strength?' and 'What was your weakness?' The candidate nearly always has more to say in answering the first question than in answering the second. Many of us apparently need to believe our own propaganda, namely that we are without serious weaknesses, or at least, that our weaknesses do not seriously impede our performance. Again and again, I have seen personal development begin for a student when he has determined to accept his own deficiencies not in the general, conventional sense of saying 'I know that I am not perfect', but in the willingness to identify particular areas of weakness. Maturity consists largely in the readiness to assess ourselves critically without destroying our self-confidence. The two fatal extremes—neither of them uncommon—is, on the one hand, the individual who must proceed on the assumption of his own superiority and infallibility; and, on the other hand, the nervous introvert who by his own misgivings has destroyed the indispensable belief in himself.

But the dividends are high and tempting for those trainees who will come to terms realistically with their own buried feelings of anxiety and inadequacy. Even the strong-minded and self-assured among us tend to resent the criticism which comes from others although it is presented tactfully and privately. Rare invitations from students and friends to 'tell me my faults' should be treated guardedly. On closer examination they prove to be requests to confirm the inflated self-image of the enquirer. But when I begin to criticize myself, that is a very different matter, full of hope and promise for improvement both for me as a person and for my performance as a leader.

This kind of introspection can have important implications for practical work with groups, as I have seen demonstrated again and again. We may learn, for example, with surprise that what is good for ourselves is not always good for the group; in other words, that we have unconsciously put the satisfaction of our own psychological needs first. Linked with this, can be a revelation about the blighting effect upon performance of our failure to understand ourselves: 'I liked her because she reminded me of my own mother', a trainee will naïvely remark of a member of a group; telling us thereby that his own feelings have kept him from seeing the facts as they truly are. But it is in the training group that failure to be objective about ourselves is most disastrous. The door is locked and bolted on the rich possibilities of training whilst we trust each other so little that we cannot bring into the open our own inadequacies. And a training group can remain for a long time in the 'slough of despond' where all contributions proceed in the belief that whatever was wrong with a piece of work it could not possibly be 'our' fault. This sentiment is seen again and again, for example, in the researches of the School of Educational Studies at the University of Sussex, which has been mentioned already.[25]

It will become clear that the leaders, too, under pressure, avoided these challenges and built up barriers to avoid them instead [p. 46]. . . . On occasions leaders had said how relieved they had been when a member had made some disapproving remark about another's behaviour; at least this had given some indication as to whether he was expected to take some action [pp. 47–8] . . . leaders become very concerned about what they felt to be their continued and unique failures, and they became inward-looking in the hope that they might be able to sort out their worries for themselves. One leader, who had not fully realized how isolated he was, expressed his feelings as follows: 'I don't seem to mind my club looking dirty or the youngsters being unruly when I'm on my own, but when other people come to visit the group, I have this sudden self-conscious feeling of appearing to be out of control and immediately want to go around the place clearing up and checking the members for the smallest thing which might be thought of as bad behaviour by the visitor' [p. 51].

In the early days of the training group, the tutor is confronted by a hidden conspiracy to avoid any discussion which brings into the open negative feelings of anxiety and personal misgivings; unconsciously, he will be expected to join the conspiracy and trainees will not always be grateful if he works to persuade them not to disown what they wish to disregard; although if the training process is successful, they too will come to see their admitted deficiencies as part of the valuable raw material at their command.

One aspect of the bold search for self-knowledge deserves detailed attention because so much has been said on the subject. We mean the place that is played in his performance by the worker's own values. A demand has grown up that he shall be 'non-judgmental'. As we shall see, this insistence relates to an insight that is faithful and true, that is linked with a professional approach and a request that we show respect for the client. But one wonders whether the demand for a 'value-free' approach has not been pressed too far until it has become a myth and a sacred cow. Perhaps there has been a confusion here between the role of the sociologist and that of the social worker. It is true, of course, that the former should be as far as is possible, 'value-free'. He is concerned to see and describe what is, rather than what ought to be. His endless and shameless curiosity makes him as interested in the activities of the criminal as in attempts to reform the criminal. But in our view, the criteria for educationalists and social workers in this matter are different. Here it would be more accurate to claim that the demand is that the operatives should be aware of the personal values they bring to the scene and, of course, by self-awareness, moderate their influence.

It would not be required to stress the point except that newcomers to social work roles—both part-time and professional—display an inclination to be oversold on this claim. Is it unfair to suggest that our enthusiasm for this notion is not entirely disinterested, being not unconnected with a desire to raise our status and that of the work we do?

The unsophisticated rapture for a new idea may be modified if, refusing to be swept along by the fashion of the hour, we ponder a few realities:

(a) Our values are a part of us and cannot be temporarily discarded like an overcoat when the sun comes out from behind the clouds. Nowhere does the argument for a 'non-judgmental' approach carry so much weight as in the sphere of detached youth work, where the youngster is met on the street, not invited into a building with an implicit assumption of the acceptance of standards. Here, if anywhere, we must 'start with them where they are' and not allow our own value system to impede our acceptance of them as they are. Yet in practice it has been found that the worker cannot discard or disregard his own personal values if he is to retain his own integrity. Let us choose one example from the many which clamour to be mentioned.

Mary Morse[26] reports on one of the workers in a project, who was prepared to go a long way with the young people he had contacted and, to retain their acceptance of him and to communicate his acceptance of them, shared activities which were not a normal part of his way of life. So he joined in the parties in the homes of members of the group whose parents were away, having no knowledge of the use to which their houses were being put. But he drew the line when, at these parties, promiscuous sexual activity took place in the bedrooms; here was an activity which he could neither condone nor share—at the risk of breaking his rapport—since it was clean contrary to his personal values.

(b) In fact, if in establishing a relationship with other human beings we feel we must suppress entirely our own convictions about right and wrong, then at best we are patronizing them and, at worst, insulting them. The implication is that we must be what we think to be less than our best in order to get alongside them, since they are lesser breeds without the law; in the telling phrase, we 'talk down to them'. A lot of woolly thinking has been heavily disguised as progressive approaches in this respect. In my view, it is an unreflecting conclusion that only uncommitted people can be effective educationalists and socialist workers. Almost the contrary seems to be true; rootless people plant few trees.

(c) In practice, all community workers, of whatever sub-species, proceed upon certain value assumptions if it be only the belief that the most wretched human being is worth helping, and has the capacity to respond to help together with a dignity and promise that may be encouraged. In a classic book on the subject, Paul Halmos has demonstrated that modern social workers, determined to be objective and detached and 'scientific', may be accused of using the disguised language of love and compassion, and even of theology.[27] But those who write from within the profession of social work also make explicit the value assumptions of their endeavours. What these are, we shall presently explore.

(d) All community work—including group work—can be dysfunctional for the personal development of the participants; the skill and insight of leaders can be used for evil as well as good purposes. Many western observers feel that in totalitarian countries, group skill is used for indoctrination, propaganda, conformity and control; that in fact these techniques have replaced the old instruments of physical torture, being less messy and far more efficient. In the 'Red Banner' factory in Leningrad I was told that a worker falling below the required level of productivity would be brought before a committee and subjected to group pressures for improvement. The guide pretended at first not to hear my further question whether these people's courts would deal with issues of personal conduct outside the factory; when I insisted he gave an evasive answer, but finally admitted that matters of private morality were also a subject for these group pressures. Of course, this interpretation might simply be a matter of western prejudice, and I would not like the present argument to be thought to rest on a political or ideological judgment. But the fact that the issue can be raised at all is sufficient to demonstrate that skill in group techniques does not of itself guarantee that the goals are right in our eyes; values are involved.

In the valuable discussion about the part played by the worker's own standards, there is a confusion which arises due to the failure to distinguish between the values themselves and the sanctions or ideologies which support those values. Thus—to go at once to the central example—community workers might rally behind a common banner which insists that everybody with whom they work is to be respected as a unique human being capable of handling his own affairs and not to be cajoled, bullied, bribed, tricked or in any way used as a means to an end which is chosen for them. But the personal philosophy which supports this common platform will vary from worker to worker.

One view will be that whatever has come about, a man is superior to the rest of the animals and his capacity for self-choosing has to be respected; another is driven by the conviction that the masses have for too long been controlled by a minority who have used power to their own advantage; whilst a third man will be on the march because he has religious convictions and holds that every single human is to be respected, to be offered the chances of education rather than be subjected to the pressures of propaganda because his ultimate status is to be part of the creative intention of an eternal God and to have the capacity for a personal relationship with Him. In this argument the dialectical opponents have not always made plain whether they are talking about the values which shape their relationship with the people they work with or the personal philosophy which supports those values; hence they often give the impression of shouting to each other across seas of misunderstanding.

But in their insistence that in some sense community workers should be 'value free' and 'non-judgmental', the advocates are warning us against real dangers and pointing us to tolerable gains.

(a) If the personal values of the community worker figure too prominently in the relationship that he encourages and the methods he uses, then there is a sizable danger that the 'client' will be tempted not to use his own experience but that of the worker; and it will appear on him like an ill-fitting suit. The recurring quotation for this possibility is that the worker may have acquired middle-class bourgeois values from his social experience—say, in his use of language and attitudes to property—which unwittingly he is superimposing on the working class values of the 'client'. Most of us are disposed to make the gratuitous, unexamined assumption that our personal values are inevitable for everybody else; but a more thoughtful assessment can prompt us to see how that is to tempt others to use our experience instead of their own.

(b) Second, the current emphasis warns us against the perpetual danger that the 'client' will become over-dependent on the worker, become fixated at a childish phase and neglect to recognize and use his own powers. Ottaway remarks:[28]

> The problem of dependency thus arises, since people tend to be dependent upon a leader and dislike taking the initiative. The group has to be weaned from dependence on the leader, and one of his first tasks is to face them with this dilemma. In a permissive group the leader does not attempt to dominate or direct. When the group becomes, to a greater or lesser degree, independent of the leader, then the members begin to share experiences more freely, and genuine communication

begins. . . . The leader does not always give the lead, and he must often be prepared to wait in silence. To tolerate silence and be prepared to wait is a valuable ability in a leader.

(c) To put the last point another way, 'our solutions are not necessarily their solutions', a trite conclusion but one that is again and again a vital discovery for the trainee. In diverse group situations there is clear evidence that the members will develop their own resources if the leader is on guard against importing his own value-system into the association.

(d) Educational norms require of the group worker—and of every other type of community worker—that he allow the values to arise from the problems, tasks and general situation which members of the group confront rather than from his personal philosophy. That is why if we listen long enough to the intervention of group leaders we can judge their calibre. Is the frequent flavour of the interventions, 'I've always said that, life has taught me that etc.', or is it, 'What do we think is involved here?'

After what the writer considers to be a required discussion of the issues raised by the demand that the group leader, and other community workers, should be 'non-judgmental', it may not be inappropriate to conclude this section by a brief summary which suggests what those values might be. First, there are professional standards and loyalties where 'professional' relates to an operative who has received specialized training for the work and earns his living thereby. And here there would be included specialized features such as values about being fair to one's employer, to one's fellow workers as well as to the profession as a whole, and the ethics about this vocation which have grown through training, practice and association. But it may cogently be argued that this is too narrow an interpretation of 'professional' and that we ought to extend its usage to cover all those who want to perform in a way that satisfies the evolving criteria of those who engage in community work. This expanded interpretation could be taken to include: (1) a conscience about always promoting the purposes for which this work exists including in our case the social adjustment and education of individuals; (2) an obligation to increase our knowledge and skill; (3) a duty to look outside the role for the satisfaction of our own major emotional satisfactions; and (4) a responsibility to maintain an attitude to the client which respects the confidentiality of anything he tells us with the wish that it should be treated in confidence; respects his right to self-determination; accepts him as he is, not allowing our own personal philosophies to erect barriers between ourselves and him. Second, our personal values are involved for behind every community worker is a human being whose true character in the end must be revealed in his relationship with members of the group; he cannot for ever play a part at the dictates, say, of a book on the techniques of the group worker; his 'unconscious' will not always be under the rational control of his 'conscious'; what he is will sometimes escape. Attempts have several times been made to depict the community worker as a 'social technician' whose motivation and values do not matter; in my view all such attempts have failed.

We only survive and sustain a good level when our efforts spring ultimately—not from a learned technique—but from a basic respect and concern for others which is part of our personality. From this fundamental requirement spring the other 'graces' which wear well in a supportive and educational role—sensitivity to the needs of others, a well-adjusted mature personality of our own, reasonable restraint and vitality.

Do the motives of leaders matter?

This topic has often been the subject of a tense session with the whole group or in a private tutorial. A well-trodden path is that a man will assume a leadership role—whether voluntary, part-time paid, or full-time professional is no matter—and make the unexamined assumption that his motives are the loftiest, that he is in fact doing this for the sake of other people. But a course of training which impels him toward a rigorous self-examination makes him uncertain about his altruism, and he comes to see that, at least, he was not quite as selfless as he supposed. (A similar re-assessment may often take place in a family circle. The mother is moderately describing how busy she is with her social work on behalf of the poor and deprived in the town; or making modest reference to her efforts on behalf of the neighbours; or claiming that, 'I work my fingers to the bone for this family.' One of the juniors may retort, 'Go on, Mum, you only do it because you enjoy doing it. You get more out of it than they do.')

At this stage, the student may be standing at the crossroads. He may take a direction leading to a psychological determinism which, because it is emotional as well as intellectual, arrives at the cynical conclusion that nobody ever wants to serve others and everybody is out for what they can get for themselves, although they will go to pains to disguise their true intentions even from themselves. Or, suffering from the shock of the self-indictment, he may give up what he has begun; or, though he may react less drastically, he can be severely discouraged.

It seems to us that the right turning at this junction is into a road which reaches a realistic and mature insight into the place of motives in human choices, although the student may need a lot of tutorial help before his feet find this road.

For most of the things that we do, there are several reasons, hence the common references to 'mixed motives'. A man marries a particular girl supremely because he wants to make that one girl happy; but he also wants to satisfy his biological drives in a socially-acceptable way; he wants to be a father; he wants to get away from home. A man goes to work to earn money, but he is careful to choose a job which will give him satisfaction which is suitable to his talents and inclination.

Do motives, then, not matter at all? Of course they do. We cannot help noticing those leaders who, in a different sense from most of the rest of us, are somehow 'in it for what they can get out of it'. In the film *Kes*, there is a long episode where the physical education teacher takes a class of boys for football practice. From the beginning it is made ludicrously, exaggeratedly clear that he is primarily motivated by the desire to indulge a private fantasy that he is an international soccer star; he cares nothing about what happens to the boys; they know this and laugh behind his back. In youth work one can occasionally observe adult workers who are self-centred; everything they do aims at their own status, prestige and prominence; actor-producers who are setting a stage on which they can shine; adult table tennis players who even though they play with members are mostly, almost exclusively, concerned to demonstrate their own skill at the game; they are all a mixture of the comic and tragic.

What then? Are we to conclude that we should never assume a helping role with others until we can be persuaded that our motives are compounded of constituent elements bright with pure selflessness? That would be a counsel of despair and inactivity. Rather, the realities of our human condition would seem to demand that we cheerfully admit that we ourselves gain somewhat—at least in emotional income—from the endeavours. On the whole, community workers who enjoy what they are doing will perform better, with more acceptance and they will almost certainly endure longer.

A number of relevant points for discussion have emerged from the many sessions about motives, and they are given here in the hope that they might possibly be of help to a reader who may be faced with the same dilemma. Although the form in which they are presented may suggest that they are solutions offered by the tutor to the student, this is not so: they are considerations which have emerged from joint exploration of the problem.

Since whatever we undertake will contain self-regarding elements, it is more relevant to ask whether we are partly moved by the desire to work for the betterment of others, in the broadest possible meaning of the phrase. In the example from the family circle quoted on page 172, it would have been sufficient for the mother to reply, 'You are quite right, of course. I get a lot out of it myself. I don't know what I should do without it. But that is not all there is to it.'

To a marked degree the motives with which we begin community work do not matter. (One inescapable exception, of course, is where a person with evil or perverse intentions joins an organization for the opportunities it will give him of doing harm to others.) But what proves decisive is whether we allow the original motives to be changed by involvement in the work. The threshold is low for entry into the building of community work but once inside, the challenges are strong; the spirits who guard the enterprise are easy to please but hard to satisfy. Many of us who take up voluntary social work are motivated at first because of something we need. A business man realizes with a shock that the making of money is becoming the touchstone of his existence. He offers himself as a voluntary worker to an organization which strives to help discharged prisoners rehabilitate themselves in society. At first 'he is out for what he can get'; he seeks 'to save his soul' or 'to preserve his humanity'. But as he goes on, he becomes more and more interested in the work for its own sake; he is invited to undertake responsibilities which have nothing directly to do with his own satisfactions; indeed, challenges emerge which he can only accept if he is willing to forget about himself; nay, paradoxically, in the actual engagement, he can only 'save his soul' and 'preserve his humanity' if he is prepared on occasions to forget about those objectives and respond to the situation.

We have overdrawn the picture and perhaps given the possibility in its purest form. But something like this can be seen to happen to many voluntary community workers; for example, to mothers who volunteer for youth work because their own children are young adults now and they have many empty hours on their hands. In the world as it is (sometimes different from what can be the imaginary world of the ethical philosophers) we may hear ourselves saying to a community worker chastened by self-discovery, 'All right you see now that your motives were not as pure as you thought they were. But do not resign on that account. Decide to do the work more and more from the right motives.' And the necessity for choice will not have to be sought; it rises unbidden again and again. For most of the time, we can both serve ourselves and serve others; our intentions are tested when we have to choose between the two.

There are students for whom this discussion has far-reaching implications for their own understanding of life and raises deep psychological and philosophical issues.[29] At the end of long sessions of sharing lie conclusions like:

(a) We are all seeking self-fulfilment. The important question is how and where we seek it. Our instinctive drives are ennobled by their uses. For example, an ardent reformer may be making a good use of his aggressiveness.

(b) To admit that there is 'a bit of self' in everything that we do need not land us in psychological hedonism, that is, the view that we seek nothing but our own pleasure. The fact that we cannot be 'selfless' need not imply that we are all by nature 'self-centred'. We can be concerned for others as well as for ourselves. In fact, the issue is further complicated because we take pleasure in another's pleasure.

(c) To be aware of our own demands is at once to be more healthy-minded and to be saved from a self-righteousness that will reduce our effectiveness and often put a barrier between ourselves and the people among whom we work.

(d) Secondary motives can happily exist side-by-side in the same well-integrated mature personality with primary motives. As Hadfield points out, a lady devoted to rescue work among fallen girls may have been attracted to the work by sexual curiosity; a barrister who believes that he is activated by the desire to help the oppressed may learn that he also searches for self-importance; a man may become a preacher to gratify his instinct for self-display.

What then? 'The recognition of such motives brings happiness and increases power.'[30] All that is now required is that these drives should be used for social ends.

These last few paragraphs may give a false impression; they may suggest that when any one of us strays into the blind-alley of doubt about motives, a few written words will help us to discern a path back to the 'sunshine' in the High Street. That is by no means always the case; it can be a deeply personal matter which requires hours of tutorial counselling.

Ten guidelines for group leaders

Nearly all leadership roles call for an ongoing process of training; they require that we grow with the job. Some men fail under responsibility and when they do they are clearly not leaders in that position. Other leaders grow weary, stale and perfunctory, and perhaps, cynical. But the best increase in stature with the passing of time and the growth of responsibility; they learn to do better what they are doing every day; they find fresh challenges in recurring duties and realize that they have always a lot to learn. At the end, we are concerned with ways in which we can encourage this process among group workers. Naturally, we have been concerned with this issue many times before; but now we want to focus attention on it and leave the emphasis where we think it ought to be.

Improvement in manual skills for simple repetitive processes occurs almost automatically and inevitably. A packer in a factory manufacturing fine bone china will arrange twenty-four saucers for firing in the same space that a novice will place twelve; and all with incredible speed. But as we have had cause several times to observe already, it is far from being the case with the growth of skill in handling personal and group relationships. Here we are concerned with personal development and the acquisition of knowledge both of which lie behind the enhancement of practical skill. Throughout, progress relies upon a rigorous self-awareness. The trainee has to ask himself searching questions; for example, how far his style is prescribed by the expectations of those he wishes to influence, and how far by his own personality traits. The soldiers who sang:

> Kiss me goodnight Sergeant-Major,
> Sergeant-Major be a mother to me,

were probably giving humorous expression to their wish to encounter more tenderness in their leaders!

It is in this context that the following ten guidelines are offered for group leaders. Entirely fortuitous is the fact that there were also Ten Commandments! Apart from every other weighty distinction, these are not brought down from the Mount, but arise, so to speak, from a careful and detailed observation of the interactions among the people in the valley below; in other words, they have no other validity than the result of one man's labours. Their general nature is explained because they claim to have a relevance for many different types of groups. And, of course, they will read as doctrinaire or perfectionist statements. But they are intended to be no more than suggestions about possible criteria of our progress; with all such statements they serve their purpose if they prompt moments of insight and should not be treated as a comprehensive account. When we fail in leadership, as all of us do, it can be useful to know in which direction we should be moving. In the language of the *Pilgrim's Progress*, they are a 'wicket gate' rather than 'yonder light'.

Effective group leaders then:

(1) Recognize the true magnitude of their task and mobilize all their resources. They do not despair prematurely but they are careful not to engage in battles they are fated to lose. But when they undertake a task they do not neglect any of their assets including the power and strength which flow from their approval and acceptance by members of the group.

(2) Understand at least as well as any other member of the group what is their own position and standing. They discern the identity given to them by members of the group; know to a nicety what is the most powerful influence defining their role—members, outside agency and self; understand the sanctions at their disposal to affect the behaviour of members of the group; grasp what methods and procedures are most likely to help the group achieve its goals and maintain itself.

(3) Rely for the respect which they need more upon the esteem they win by the way they perform their role than on the prestige which is theirs by virtue of the office they hold. Effective leaders do not normally 'pull-rank', but aim to depend upon their usefulness to the group speaking for itself; if appointed from outside they look to be accepted within as natural indigenous leaders.

(4) Grasp at least as well as anybody else on the scene the total situation of the group. What brought them together? What do they hope to achieve? What are their norms? How far are they affected by outside factors? What has happened to their association in its history so far?

(5) Know themselves with a measure of objectivity which leads them to be neither unduly elated by praise nor unreasonably deflated by criticism. They have minimized their illusions about themselves. They have left about no land-mines which, in the traffic of interaction, may explode and blow up their comfortable self-image. They have come to terms with the realities of their own strength and weakness.

(6) Cheerfully admit what they themselves gain in emotional income from their leadership position; they do not suffer the kind of super-ego pressures which desire them to produce a selfless reason for all their actions; but are not looking to the group for the satisfaction of their major emotional needs.

(7) Grow more sensitive to other people and their developing personalities; move further and further away from an egocentricity where they do not find the experiences of others are real to them and do not fully appreciate the effect of their actions on others. Sometimes in an early session of a new class I tell an abbreviated version of a short story by Nathaniel Hawthorne[31] and invite comments: a scientist was disturbed by a blemish on his wife's face and asked her to allow him to experiment to produce a potion which would remove it. Reluctantly, the wife agreed. After much experimentation, he produced the potion in his laboratory and he induced his wife to drink it. To his delight and her surprise, an hour later the blemish on her face disappeared completely; but that same night she died from the effects of drinking the potion.

Of course, we have comments which look at the scientific possibility of the experiment. There is not a pass or fail mark in this exercise. But one or more students can be trusted to turn up with the answers from the perspective of human relationships and then the process begins of increasing our sensitivity through group interaction and problem solving. Some of the general principles emerging from the story are:

(a) How far should any one of us ever try to change another human being?

(b) Should any of us ever try to decide an important issue for another, however close they are to us? Is that not simply a case of possession?

(c) Ought we not to accept others as they are?

(d) Are human relationships often damaged because we settle on one feature of another person and focus all our attention on that?

(e) Is physical appearance often allowed too large an influence in the shaping of human relationships?

(8) Learn to communicate and co-operate with mounting effectiveness. Lack of communication is easily the most frequent criticism students have of the organizations where they go for practical work; typical of hundreds of such comments is the following:

> Each level of members of this organization interacted with very restricted groups. The two teachers communicated very little with the remainder of the group and whenever they did it would be with either the nuns or the housemothers; in fact all of the above groups associated with each other on the same pattern—one up, one down.

Two 'dogmas' emerge from the mass of material at our disposal. Leaders who both care what happens to others and wish to be productive reach a high level of communication with their colleagues and clientele. Effective leaders are more likely to spread the work load and delegate real responsibility to those on the lower rungs of the hierarchical ladder.

(9) Have a sense of timing which prompts them to act appropriately. Lenin wrote:[32]

> November sixth will be too early. We must have an all-Russian basis for the rising; and on the sixth all the delegates to the Congress will not have arrived. . . . On the other hand, November eighth will be too late. By that time the Congress will be organised, and it is difficult for a large organised body of people to take swift, decisive action. We must act on the seventh.

(10) Respond to the changing moods, dynamics and constellations of the group since they listen attentively and have the flexibility to change course when required.

Notes and references

1 Group work for everybody

1 For a good account of the relationships which develop in a team playing a competitive game see William F. Whyte (1948), *Street Corner Society*, University of Chicago Press.

2 This last illustration is suggested by Michael S. Olmsted (1959), *The Small Group*, Random House. This short book is useful for the whole of this section.

3 Adam Curle, 'Dynamics of group work', in Peter Kuenstler (ed.) (1955), *Social Group Work in Great Britain*, Faber, ch. 7, p. 148.

4 See S. H. Foulkes and E. J. Anthony (1957), *Group Psychotherapy*, Penguin.

5 For a relevant discussion see Joan E. Matthews (1966), *Working with Youth Groups*, University of London Press, chs. 1 and 3. She quotes Grace Coyle as saying in 1951 that in the United States, social group work was recognized as a basic method of social work and that its distinguishing characteristic is that the group worker uses the social relationships within the 'client's' group experience as a means of individual growth and development.

6 See A. K. C. Ottaway (1966), *Learning Through Group Experience*, Routledge & Kegan Paul.

7 See L. Button (1971), *Discovery and Experience*, Oxford University Press; a comprehensive, although rather personal, book on this subject.

2 What is happening in groups?

1 Significantly, in the story of The Prodigal Son (Luke 15:11–32), it was while he was a great way off that his father recognized him.

2 Joan E. Matthews (1961), *Training in Professional Skill*; a pamphlet published by the National Association of Youth Clubs, p. 3.

3 See L. Button (1971), *Discovery and Experience*, Oxford University Press, p. 140.

4 J. B. Priestley (1964), *Time and the Conways: Play*, Heinemann Educational.

5 P. L. Berger (1966), *Invitation to Sociology*, Penguin, p. 29.

6 In the examples quoted it is not always the case that a full verbatim account has been given but only what is thought to be useful. In some cases, the material has been rewritten in a shorter form.

7　Josephine Klein (1961), *Working with Groups*, Hutchinson, p. 51.
8　George C. Homans (1951), *The Human Group*, Routledge & Kegan Paul, pp. 123–4.
9　Ralph Linton (1936), *The Study of Man*, Appleton-Century-Crofts, p. 181.
10　C. A. Gibb (ed.) (1969), *Leadership*, Penguin, pp. 10–11.
11　Rudyard Kipling (1929), *The Complete Stalky and Company*, Macmillan, pp. 297–325.
12　J. M. Barrie (1967), *The Admirable Crichton*, University of London Press.
13　William Golding (1954), *Lord of the Flies*, Faber. There are many more works of fiction which when they have been read for enjoyment can be subjected to the same process to gain insight into group behaviour. Examples are: Charles Dickens, *Oliver Twist*, Penguin (Oliver asking for 'more'; Fagin training the young pickpockets); Jane Austen, *Sense and Sensibility*, Penguin; Barry Hines (1969), *The Blinder*, Penguin; Muriel Spark (1969), *The Prime of Miss Jean Brodie*, Penguin; and Somerset Maugham's short stories including 'Rain', 'The three fat women of Antibes', 'The force of circumstances' and 'A marriage of convenience', in W. Somerset Maugham (1963), *Collected Short Stories*, Penguin.
14　This is a shortened version from Joan E. Matthews (1966), *Working with Youth Groups*, University of London Press, pp. 52–3; see also George W. Goetschius and Joan M. Tash (1968), *Working with Unattached Youth*, Routledge & Kegan Paul, pp. 172–3.
15　Josephine Klein (1963), *Human Behaviour and Personal Relations*, National Association of Youth Clubs, p. 36.
16　Such a list may be found in L. Button, op. cit., pp. 302–3.
17　For the full account see Joan E. Matthews, op. cit., ch. 2.
18　For a truly comprehensive account of researches into small group behaviour, see D. Cartwright and Alvin Zander (eds) (1968), *Group Dynamics*, Tavistock, pp. 50ff. A useful volume in this area is George C. Homans, op. cit. He bases his conclusions on five classic pieces of research undertaken by other investigators.
19　William F. Whyte (1948), *Street Corner Society*, University of Chicago Press.
20　See the account in Michael S. Olmsted (1959), *The Small Group*, Random House, pp. 38ff.
21　A. K. C. Ottaway (1966), *Learning Through Group Experience*, Routledge & Kegan Paul.
22　A short and clear account is in J. A. C. Brown (1954), *Social Psychology and Industry*, Penguin.
23　See also W. R. Bion (1961), *Experiences in Groups*, Tavistock;

W. F. Cleugh (1962), *Educating Older People*, Tavistock; A. K. Rice (1965), *Learning for Leadership*, Tavistock.

24 See George C. Homans, op. cit.

25 See D. Cartwright and Alvin Zander (eds), op. cit., ch. 3: 'Group cohesiveness', and the five subsequent chapters which give an account of the researches on which these conclusions are based.

26 See Alex Bavelas, 'Communication patterns in task-orientated groups', in D. Cartwright and Alvin Zander (eds), op. cit., ch. 35.

27 See J. Moreno (1934), *Who Shall Survive?* Beacon House.

28 See C. A. Gibb (ed.), op, cit. and Alvin Gouldner (1950), *Studies in Leadership*, Russell.

3 Observation

1 George C. Homans (1951), *The Human Group*, Routledge & Kegan Paul, p. 434.

2 From Joan E. Matthews (1966), *Working with Youth Groups*, University of London Press, p. 25.

3 Margaret Phillips (1965), *Small Social Groups in England*, Methuen: 'A group is limited in its development by the physical conditions under which it lives and works, but can at the same time shape the conditions of its own needs' (p. 285). The tables in ibid., pp. 285–7, a summary of Phillips's conclusions, are valuable for the whole of this section.

4 For a useful discussion see Peter Worsley (ed.) (1970), *Introducing Sociology*, Penguin, pp. 219–43.

5 T. Burns and G. M. Stalker (1961), *The Management of Innovations*, Tavistock.

6 See Margaret Phillips, op. cit., p. 286: 'Informal group structure developing within an institution may represent a compromise between the purposes of the institution and the needs of the group members and may serve both.'

7 For an absorbing account see K. Ishwaran (1968), *Shivapur. A South Indian Village*, Routledge & Kegan Paul.

8 See Alex Bavelas, 'Communication patterns in task-orientated groups', in D. Cartwright and Alvin Zander (eds) (1968), *Group Dynamics*, Tavistock, ch. 35, pp. 669ff. For an account of the way in which communication systems can be imposed, see W. J. H. Sprott (1958), *Human Groups*, Penguin, ch. 8.

9 See E. E. Jennings (1960), *An Anatomy of Leadership*, Harper, p. 2.

10 R. L. Stevenson, *Virginibus Puerisque*, vi, *El Dorado*.

11 The distinction emerges clearly when there is a clash of expectations between the 'Task-oriented' and the 'Interaction-oriented'. Educationists and social workers who run pre-school groups in Hong Kong are chiefly concerned about the social

education of the children. But they receive many complaints from parents who consider that their children do not receive enough instruction in reading, writing and arithmetic.

12 This is a major theme in the final chapter of this book.

13 'Activities' and 'friendship patterns' have been a major concern in the researches of L. Button (1971), *Discovery and Experience*, Oxford University Press, ch. 4.

14 L. Button, op. cit., pp. 213ff.: other schedules on pp. 202ff. More material can be found in Joan E. Matthews, op. cit., pp. 134–40; Josephine Klein (1961), *Working with Groups*, pp. 198–214; and Margaret Phillips, op. cit., ch. 1; A. K. C. Ottaway (1966), *Learning Through Group Experience*, Routledge & Kegan Paul, ch. 6.

15 William F. Whyte (1948), *Street Corner Society*, University of Chicago Press, pp. 333ff.

16 In D. Cartwright and Alvin Zander (eds), op. cit., there is a list in the index of methods of observation for both experimental and field studies. Some of them are mathematical systems. See also R. F. Bales (1951), *Interaction Process Analysis*, Addison-Wesley. Bales recorded and counted each action by and to each member. He found that about 45 per cent of actions were directed to the man who was ranked first; 18 per cent to the one ranked second and about 6 per cent to the lowest in the ranking. And whatever the size of the group, whether from 3 to 8, the basic pattern was the same.

17 What follows is a brief summary of R. F. Bales, op. cit.

18 See Josephine Klein, op. cit., for these and for an impressive application of Bales's discoveries.

19 Karen Horney (1937), *The Neurotic Personality of Our Time*, Routledge & Kegan Paul.

20 To carry this topic further the reader is advised to read W. R. Bion (1961), *Experience in Groups*, Tavistock. The underlying theme of this famous work is that there are unconscious, basic assumptions behind the behaviour of the group—of dependence, pairing, fight-or-flight—which influence the choice of the leader and other matters.

21 Josephine Klein, op. cit., ch. 4.

22 The term 'community worker' is used here to mean all those people in whatever setting, and full-time, part-time and voluntary, who work with people in the broadest sense for their 'betterment'.

23 See the 'Gulbenkian Report' (1968), *Community Work and Social Change*, Longmans; and R. A. B. Leaper (1968), *Community Work*, N.C.S.S.

24 For adolescents as a social group see Fred Milson (1972), *Youth in a Changing Society*, Routledge & Kegan Paul.

25 See, for example, Department of Education and Science (1969),
   Youth and Community Work in the 70s, HMSO.
26 Department of Education and Science (1967), *Children and their
   Primary Schools* (Plowden Report), HMSO.
27 Typical of early efforts at recording is the work of a first-year
   student on which I have written the comment: 'This is fascinating
   stuff. Of course, you have the evidence for these views. But you
   do not give any of it.' It read like a Dickens novel with
   brilliant characterization but I suspect that he had been swept
   along by his own powerful imagination!

4 Interpretation

1 Many examples are provided in what is surely Freud's most
   readable work: *The Psychopathology of Everyday Life* (1966),
   Benn. See also David Stafford-Clark (1967), *What Freud Really
   Said*, Pelican, ch. 4. The quotations which follow are taken from
   this book.
2 George Mead (1971), 'Self', in Kenneth Thompson and Jeremy
   Tunstall (eds), *Sociological Perspectives*, Penguin, p. 148. The
   whole paper (chapter 10) is worth reading at this point.
3 And I record as a fact that in my extensive sample, there is a
   marked trend for the women students to be 'more person-
   orientated and less group-orientated' than the men students.
4 Michael Argyle (1967), *The Psychology of Interpersonal Behaviour*,
   Penguin. The present quotation is taken from chapter 1: 'Social
   motivation', but the whole book is valuable for this stage of the
   training. See in particular chapter 7: 'Self-image and self-
   esteem', and chapter 6: 'Eye-contact and the direction of the gaze'.
5 I owe this illustration to Peter Worsley (1970), *Introducing
   Sociology*, Penguin, pp. 216ff., but I have adapted it to our
   present purpose. Worsley acknowledges his own debt to William
   F. Whyte (1948), *Human Relations in the Restaurant Industry*,
   McGraw-Hill.
6 Although in chapter 3 we have described the rationale and the
   means for estimating the effect of wider social and cultural
   factors upon the whole group.
7 And a good chapter providing useful background material for this
   subject, is chapter 3 of Michael S. Olmsted (1959), *The Small
   Group*, Random House.
8 Cyril Smith, 'Problems in the classroom teaching of social group
   method', privately circulated working paper.
9 J. A. Davis, 'Composition effects, role systems and the survival
   of small discussion groups', in A. P. Hare, *et al.* (1961), *Small
   Groups*, Knopf.

10 George C. Homans (1951), *The Human Group*, Routledge &
Kegan Paul, p. 60.

11 See *inter alia*, D. Cartwright and Alvin Zander (eds) (1968),
Group Dynamics, Tavistock, part 2: 'Group cohesiveness', p. 72:
Obviously several different things are included in these intuitive
operational descriptions of group cohesiveness. At least three
rather different meanings may be distinguished:
(a) Attraction to the group, including resistance to leaving it;
(b) Motivation of the members to participate in group activities;
(c) Co-ordination of the efforts of the members.

12 Antony Jay (1972), *The Corporation Man*, Michael Joseph.

13 George J. McCall and J. L. Simmons (1966), *Identities and
Interaction*, Collier-Macmillan.

14 For this whole passage, we are indebted to Michael Argyle, op.
cit., ch. 2. Once again the reader is recommended to read this
book, which while having a scholarly competence, still satisfies
the education criterion that 'it helps us to realize what we
already know'.

15 L. Button (1971), *Discovery and Experience*, Oxford University
Press, p. 88.

16 A. K. C. Ottaway (1966), *Learning Through Group Experience*,
Routledge & Kegan Paul, p. 140; in fact the whole chapter—
'Personal reports'—is rewarding at this stage of the argument.

17 Youth Service Research Project (1969), *The Use of Group
Discussion Methods in the Training of Part-time Voluntary Club
Leaders*, School of Educational Studies, University of Sussex,
p. 53. This project was presented to the Department of Education
and Science.

18 See Alan F. Sillitoe (1959), *The Loneliness of the Long-Distance
Runner*, W. H. Allen.

19 A. K. C. Ottaway, op. cit., p. 124.

20 L. Button, op. cit., p. 155.

21 2 Samuel 11:12.

22 Luke 15:1–2.

23 For a plentiful supply of useful information see George
Goetschius and Joan M. Tash (1968), *Working with Unattached
Youth*, Routledge & Kegan Paul.

24 See F. S. Haiman (1951), *Group Leadership and Democratic
Action*, Houghton Mifflin, ch. 4, p. 181; Margaret Phillips (1965),
Small Social Groups in England, Methuen; and George W.
Goetschius and Joan M. Tash, op. cit.

5   Action

1 Youth Service Research Project (1969), *The Use of Group
Discussion Methods in the Training of Part-time Voluntary Club*

Leaders, School of Educational Studies, University of Sussex, p. 53, presented to the Department of Education and Science.

2 L. Button (1971), *Discovery and Experience*, Oxford University Press, p. 67.

3 George C. Homans (1951), *The Human Group*, Routledge & Kegan Paul.

4 Michael Argyle (1967), *The Psychology of Interpersonal Behaviour*, Penguin.

5 Doris Odlum (1957), *Journey Through Adolescence*, Delisle, p. 47.

6 T. R. Batten (1967), *The Non-Directive Approach in Group and Community Work*, Oxford University Press. In the last chapter on 'Leadership' there is a more detailed examination of this question.

7 In the field of social education a mass of case material is available on request from the Youth Service Information Centre, 37, Belvoir Street, Leicester. See also L. Button, op. cit., pp. 210–15; Joan E. Matthews (1966), *Working with Youth Groups*, University of London Press, ch. 9; and Margaret Phillips (1965), *Small Social Groups in England*, Methuen.

8 F. S. Haiman (1951), *Group Leadership and Democratic Action*, Houghton Mifflin, pp. 176–7.

9 George W. Goetschius and Joan M. Tash (1968), *Working with Unattached Youth*, Routledge & Kegan Paul, pp. 194–8.

10 Quoted in John Bazalgette (1971), *Freedom Authority and the Young Adult*, Pitman, p. 50.

11 See F. S. Haiman (1951), *Group Leadership and Democratic Action*, Houghton Mifflin, p. 194. See also Home Office (1966), *Groupwork in Probation*; Howard Jones (1962), 'The Group Approach to Treatment', *Howards Journal*, 2, 1; Howard Jones (1970), *Crime in a Changing Society*, Penguin.

12 George W. Goetschius and Joan M. Tash, op. cit.

13 See Josephine Klein (1961), *Working with Groups*, Hutchinson, ch. 5; and S. H. Foulkes and E. J. Anthony (1957), *Group Psychotherapy*, Penguin.

14 Josephine Klein, op. cit., p. 62.

15 Ibid., pp. 54–5.

16 A. K. C. Ottaway (1966), *Learning Through Group Experience*, Routledge & Kegan Paul, p. 100. Chapter 5 contains many illustrations of the present theme on the therapy of small groups and the need for individuals to relive their early experience.

17 L. Button, op. cit., p. 147.

18 See *inter alia* Grace Coyle (1948), *Group Work with American Youth*, Harper.

19 L. Button, op. cit., p. 152.

20 A. K. Rice (1965), *Learning for Leadership*, Tavistock, p. 158.

21 F. S. Haiman, op. cit., p. 181. This section owes a lot to Haiman.
22 See Howard Jones, op. cit., ch. 9: 'Criminals in captivity'.
23 See in particular T. R. Batten, op. cit., and (1970), *The Human Factor in Youth Work*, Oxford University Press.
24 See Fred Milson (1970), *Youth Work in the 1970s*, Routledge & Kegan Paul.
25 See Ronald Goldman (1969), *Angry Adolescents*, Routledge & Kegan Paul.
26 John Leigh (1971), *Young People and Leisure*, Routledge & Kegan Paul.
27 John Bazalgette, op. cit.
28 I have written a more detailed account with scripts for practice in a booklet: *Role Playing as a Youth Club Activity*, Methodist Youth Department.

6 Leadership

1 Thomas Carlyle (1840), *On Heroes, Hero-Worship and the Heroic in History*, Crowell, pp. 20–1.
2 Frederick Thrasher (1927), *The Gang*, University of Chicago Press.
3 Henry L. Smith and L. M. Krueger (1949), *A Brief Summary of Literature on Leadership*, vol. 9, Bulletin of the School of Education, Indiana University.
4 See C. A. Gibb (ed.) (1969), *Leadership*, Penguin.
5 Alex Bavelas, 'Communication patterns in task-orientated groups', in D. Cartwright and Alvin Zander (eds) (1968), *Group Dynamics*, Tavistock publications, ch. 35; C. A. Gibb, op. cit., pp. 20–31.
6 Karl Mannheim (1936), *Ideology and Utopia*, Routledge & Kegan Paul.
7 T. W. Adorno, Else Frenkel-Brunswick, D. J. Levinson, and R. N. Sandford (1950), *The Authoritarian Personality*, Harper.
8 For this section see Alvin Gouldner (ed.) (1950), *Studies in Leadership*, Harper.
9 See *New Society*, 257, p. 284.
10 William Shakespeare, *Othello*, Iago to Roderigo, Act 1, Scene 1, line 43.
11 See Geoffrey Moorhouse (1971), *Calcutta*, Weidenfeld & Nicolson.
12 Ibid., p. 347.
13 Kimball Young (1944), *Social Psychology*, Appleton-Century-Crofts, p. 222.
14 Vance Packard (1959), *The Status Seekers*, Penguin, p. 23.
15 The liability of members of small groups to develop attitudes of dependence is brought out in W. R. Bion (1961), *Experiences in Groups*, Tavistock, p. 84:

Complaints will be made that my remarks are too theoretical; that they are mere intellectualizations; that my manner lacks warmth; that I am too abstract. . . . I shall now suggest that all facets of behaviour in the dependent groups can be recognized as related if we suppose that in this group power is believed to flow not from science but from magic. One of the characteristics demanded of the leader of the group, then, is that he should either be a magician or behave like one.

16 *The Memoirs of Field-Marshal the Viscount Montgomery of Alamein, K.G.* (1958), Collins.

17 Elizabeth Longford (1969), *Wellington—The Years of the Sword*, Weidenfeld & Nicolson, p. 322.

18 Antony Jay (1961), *Management and Machiavelli*, Hodder & Stoughton.

19 M. G. Ross and C. E. Hendry (1957), *New Understanding of Leadership*, Association Press. Students also find an intriguing description of 'father' and 'mother' type leaders in Margaret Phillips (1965), *Small Social Groups in England*, Methuen.

20 David Riesman (1958), *The Lonely Crowd*, Doubleday.

21 John F. Kennedy (1965) *Profiles in Courage*, Hamish Hamilton, p. 26.

22 Hans Gerth and C. Wright Mills (1954), *Character and Social Structure*, Routledge & Kegan Paul, ch. 14: 'The sociology of leadership'.

23 C. A. Gibb (ed.), op. cit., p. 205.

24 L. Button (1971), *Discovery and Experience*, Oxford University Press, pp. 88–90.

25 Youth Service Research Project (1969), *The Use of Group Discussion Methods in the Training of Part-time Voluntary Club Leaders*, School of Educational Studies, University of Sussex, presented to the Department of Education and Science.

26 Mary Morse (1965), *The Unattached*, Penguin.

27 Paul Halmos (1965), *The Faith of the Counsellors*, Constable.

28 A. K. C. Ottaway (1966), *Learning Through Group Experience*, Routledge & Kegan Paul, pp. 15 and 17.

29 Although I need to resist the temptation to refer students to books for an answer to their perplexities, I should not fail to mention that there is one chapter which has often proved of practical help in this matter: J. A. Hadfield (1923), *Psychology and Morals*, Methuen, ch. 22: 'Motives: selfish and altruistic'.

30 Ibid., p. 203.

31 Nathaniel Hawthorne (1872), 'The elixir of life', *Atlantic Monthly*.

32 John Reed (1966), *Ten Days That Shook The World*, Penguin, p. 73.

Suggestions for further reading

Argyle, Michael (1967), *The Psychology of Interpersonal Behaviour*, Penguin.

Berger, Peter L. (1966), *Invitation to Sociology*, Penguin.

Berger, Peter L. (1971), *A Rumour of Angels*, Penguin.

Bronowski, J. (1967), *The Identity of Man*, Penguin.

Button, L. (1971), *Discovery and Experience*, Oxford University Press.

Cartwright, D. and Zander, Alvin (1968), *Group Dynamics*, Tavistock.

Gibb, C. A. (ed.) (1969), *Leadership*, Penguin: Modern Psychology Series.

Homans, G. C. (1951), *The Human Group*, Routledge & Kegan Paul.

Klein, Josephine (1961), *Working with Groups*, Hutchinson.

Kuenstler, Peter (ed.) (1955), *Social Group Work in Great Britain*, Faber.

Lewin, K. (1953), *Field Theory in Social Science*, Tavistock.

Matthews, Joan E. (1966), *Working with Youth Groups*, University of London Press.

Olmsted, Michael S. (1959), *The Small Group*, Random House.

Ottaway, A. K. C. (1966), *Learning Through Group Experience*, Routledge & Kegan Paul.

Phillips, Margaret (1965), *Small Social Groups in England*, Methuen.

Sprott, W. J. H. (1958), *Human Groups*, Penguin.

Whyte, William F. (1948), *Street Corner Society*, University of Chicago Press.

Subject index

Author index